Gareth Jenkins

Context and Circumstance: The Turkish Military and Politics

Adelphi Paper 337

Published in the United States
by Routledge

First published February 2001 by **Routledge**
2 Park Square, Milton Park, Abingdon, Oxon, OX14 4RN

Transferred to Digital Printing 2005

Director John Chipman
Editor Mats R. Berdal
Project Manager, Design and Production Mark Taylor

British Library Cataloguing in Publication Data
Data available

Library of Congress Cataloguing in Publication Data

ISBN 0-19-850971-5
ISSN 0567-932x

Contents

Introduction

Over the last decade Turkey has been the focus of more international, particularly Western, attention than at any time in the republic's history.[1] The new security environment has enhanced, rather than diminished, Turkey's economic and strategic importance to the US. While the increasingly close relationship between the EU and Ankara, which culminated in December 1999 in Turkey's inclusion in the list of candidates for accession, has focused European attention not only on the country's foreign relations but on whether its domestic policies comply with the Copenhagen criteria for EU membership.

To most proponents of the Western model of liberal representative democracy, the continued domination of Turkish politics by the country's military appears to be an anomalous anachronism, even an anathema. As a result, discussions of civil–military relations often become coloured by moral judgments as military involvement in politics is seen as not only undesirable but almost an affront to a natural order. The purpose of this paper is neither to condemn nor to justify the Turkish military's involvement in politics; merely to try to understand and explain. It attempts to answer three basic questions:

- Why does the military exercise such influence in Turkey?
- How does the military exercise such influence?
- What are the implications of the military's influence for Turkey's domestic and foreign security policies both now and into the future?

The paper argues that the role of the military in Turkey is rooted in Turkish society, history and culture. The military has always lain at the heart of how Turks define themselves; and most still regard the institution of the military as the embodiment of the highest virtues of the nation.[2]

The resultant high public esteem in which the military is held has been enhanced, rather than eroded, by the Turkish experience of multi-party democracy. Even its detractors admit that the Turkish military is not only the most efficient institution in Turkey but has remained relatively free of the corruption that has become endemic in both the government and the civil service. Even given the low standing of politicians worldwide, Turkish politicians have a poor reputation, being almost universally regarded as venal, incompetent, unprincipled and self-serving. On several occasions in recent Turkish history, political infighting has brought the machinery of government close to collapse. In such situations it has been to the military that the Turkish public has tended to turn, either to intervene directly or to provide leadership in applying pressure to the government.[3]

Yet the public mandate for an interventionist role in politics does not extend to support for military rule. Few Turks have pleasant memories of the two occasions when the military has taken over the government of the country.[4] This is particularly true of the most recent period of military rule, 1980–83, which is remembered as being oppressive and restrictive, even though the September 1980 coup that preceded it was welcomed at the time for restoring order and saving the country from a potentially bloody civil war.[5]

The Turkish military's role as a 'moderating power',[6] responsible for protecting the country against squabbling civilian politicians, has parallels elsewhere.[7] But the Turkish military is unusual in that it has traditionally been reluctant either to seize power or to participate in the civilian administration. If possible, it has preferred to remain aloof from day-to-day politics, which it tends to regard as debased and debasing. Although its pension fund, known by its Turkish acronym of OYAK,[8] has major shareholdings in several companies,[9] it has remained organisationally distinct from the military itself, which has made little attempt to develop its own economic interests.[10]

But what makes the Turkish military unique is that it sees itself as having an almost sacred duty to protect an indigenous ideology,[11] namely Kemalism, the principles laid down by the founder of the Turkish republic, Kemal Ataturk. This ideological dimension to the military's perception of its role has meant that its definition of security extends beyond public order and Turkey's political or economic interests to include threats to the country's Kemalist legacy.

Kemalism is enshrined in the Turkish constitution and includes a rigorous commitment to secularism, territorial integrity and cultural homogeneity. Over the last 30 years Kemalism has been taught with an increasing intensity in both civilian schools and military academies, initially in an attempt to create an ideological bulwark against communism, but more recently to counter the two most dynamic ideological forces of the post-Cold War world, radical Islam and fissiparous nationalism, which in Turkey has meant Kurdish separatism. It was in response to these perceived threats to Kemalism that the Turkish military returned to the political arena during the 1990s.[12]

Yet the military's influence on policy is neither uniform nor total. It only attempts to exert influence in areas with, by its own definition, a security dimension. For example, it has shown little interest in economic policy.[13]

Military influence over policy also depends on the degree to which it differs with the government over a specific issue. For example, it is unusual for there to be a divergence of opinion over foreign affairs, which tend to be seen as state rather than government or party policy. As a result, although the military closely monitors foreign policy, it has less need to intervene to try to influence it.

When it does attempt to influence policy, the military depends on its informal authority, based on a combination of its historical role and its public prestige, rather than any officially defined legislative or executive powers. In theory, the military is not only subject to civilian control – it is subordinate to the prime ministry – but the main platform on which it attempts to exercise influence, the National Security Council (NSC), is merely an advisory body which reports to the Council of Ministers.

In practice, however, the military's informal authority is such that, when it expresses an opinion, civilian governments rarely try to implement a policy which contradicts it. Yet the military has proved less successful in persuading governments actively to initiate policy.

The result is a system in which civilian authority is primary, rather than supreme, and where the military is able to prevent policy from straying outside specific parameters, rather than making things happen within them.

Ironically, it is the prospect of fulfilling Ataturk's greatest dream that now presents the military with its greatest dilemma. The overriding aim of Ataturk's ambitious reform programme[14] of the 1920s and 1930s was to transform Turkey into a modern, Western state able to take its place on equal terms in the European family of nations. Today that means joining the EU. But the Europe that Ataturk so assiduously imitated no longer exists. Not only are today's EU members expected to cede a measure of sovereignty to Brussels but, as the EU made clear in November 2000,[15] Turkish membership would require the radical reform of several of the keystones of the Kemalist state, including the withdrawal of the military from the political arena and the lifting of restrictions on political and cultural pluralism; concessions which the military fears could eventually lead to the establishment of a separate Kurdish or even Islamist state.

Chapter 1

The Military and Turkish Society

The political role of the military in Turkey has grown out of a specifically Turkish historical, social and cultural context. But the military's pre-eminent role in Turkish life is not merely a historical hangover. Not only is Turkish society still dominated by the values, attitudes and traditions which underpin the role of the military but, to the vast majority of Turks, the military and military values still lie at the heart of any definition of what it means to be Turkish.

Ironically, the role of the military has been enhanced rather than eroded by Turks' experience of parliamentary democracy. The failure of parliamentary democracy to provide prosperity, efficient government or political stability brought the military back into the political arena in the 1950s and has subsequently created a broad, though not universal, public mandate for an interventionist role in the political process as the guarantor of last resort of stability and public order.

The military's role is further bolstered by public perceptions of the security environment, where external and internal threats are often inflated and distorted by conspiracy theories in which even Turkey's NATO allies are secretly plotting to weaken and divide the country.[1] In such a situation, it is to the military that most Turks turn, not only as the protector of Turkey's territory and economic and political interests but as the guardian of the state ideology of Kemalism.

The Historical Context

The military has always played a central role in Turkish history. The Turks' first appearance in history, when they emerged from Central Asia, was as an army rather than a nation. The Ottoman Empire too was 'an army before it was anything else',[2] created through conquest and, particularly initially, administered along military lines. It has even been argued that both the structure of the state and Ottoman society itself were 'auxiliary elements for the support of the armed forces'.[3]

During the nineteenth century, as the Ottoman Empire entered its final decline, the military was in the vanguard of attempts to create a modern Western state,[4] not only importing Western military theories and technology, but also establishing the first secular schools for Muslims, publishing the first-ever Turkish grammars[5] and even pioneering the simplification of the Turkish script which led eventually to the adoption of the Latin alphabet.[6]

In 1908, in what became known in the West as the 'Young Turks Revolution', a group of Ottoman officers seized power and forced the Sultan to introduce constitutional rule. Following defeat in the First World War it was a military officer Mustafa Kemal, later to be known as Ataturk, who not only drove out an invading Greek army and the occupying Allied forces during what is known in Turkey as the War of Liberation, but in 1923 created the modern Turkish Republic.

Although Ataturk resigned from the military to become Turkey's first president, a post he held until his death in 1938, it was his status as a military hero which gave him the authority to push through a series of radical reforms in an attempt to transform the rump of the Ottoman Empire into a homogenous, Western-style modern nation state.

Ataturk established a political party, the Republican People's Party (RPP), which enjoyed a monopoly of power until 1950.[7] He also insisted that all officers who wished to participate in politics should resign from the armed forces. The result was to remove the military as an institution from the political arena, although until 1950 virtually all of the leading politicians were Ataturk's former military colleagues from the War of Liberation and Turkey was effectively ruled by former soldiers in civilian clothes.[8]

In the 1950 general election the conservative Democrat Party (DP) won a landslide victory over the RPP, ending the era of single-party rule. The DP Chairman Adnan Menderes became prime minister and remained in power for the rest of the decade. From the outset, Menderes pursued a populist agenda, in which policy was shaped by short-term political advantage. The result was an increase in political instability, which was exacerbated by Menderes' increasing authoritarianism as he attempted to restrict the activities of the RPP and establish a virtual single-party dictatorship. In 1960, amid growing public unrest, the Menderes government was toppled by Turkey's first military coup.[9]

Civilian rule was reintroduced in 1961, only for the military to stage a second coup in 1971 when infighting between the political parties represented in parliament brought the machinery of government to a standstill.

On 12 September 1980, as street fighting between leftist and rightist extremists brought the country to the brink of civil war, the military staged a third coup. This time it remained in power for three years. In 1982 the military issued a new constitution, which remains in force today, before allowing a return to civilian rule in 1983.

The Social and Cultural Context

Turks, like their language, are agglutinative,[10] with a strong sense of group membership and a concomitant almost instinctive awareness of an obligation to provide assistance to others when required. By Western standards, individualism is very rare.

Turkish society tends to be hierarchical, patriarchal and authoritarian, with an emphasis on collective rather than individual rights and values. The result is a society which is both more cohesive and more restrictive than those in Western democracies. But both the cohesion and the restrictions owe more to traditional values and social pressure than to legislation.

For most Turks, communal integrity takes precedence over individual rights and freedoms, whether in the family, the broader local community or the nation. Such attitudes are reinforced by the education system, which explicitly inculcates the concept of the individual as merely a component of a greater whole, initially as a member of the extended family but ultimately of the Turkish nation.

Turkish primary school children are taught that 'society is like a huge family',[11] 'love of the motherland is the supreme human emotion'[12] and 'humans cannot live without a motherland.'[13] They are exhorted to dedicate their lives to the nation by swearing: 'Let my life be a gift to the existence of Turkishness'.[14]

Pluralism, whether personal or political, is often viewed with suspicion as posing a potential threat to social or national cohesion. Turkish children are taught that 'one of the elements that makes the Turkish nation is the subordination of the individual's own interests to those of the nation'[15] and that 'societies which fail to instil unity and togetherness cannot live as a nation; they are broken up and destroyed.'[16]

Personal relations within both the family and in the broader community are usually based on the exchange of loyalty and patronage, and characterised by extreme deference to authority. Turks' sense of occupying a specific place in a hierarchy is reinforced by the education system, which teaches that: 'One of the special characteristics of the Turkish race is respect for those above one and love for those below,'[17] and 'Social harmony is dependent on this respect and love.'[18]

Although verbal complaints are commonplace, actual challenges to authority, or the questioning of its abuse, whether in the family or the broader community, are rare and sustained challenges even rarer.

The subordination of the individual to the nation is reinforced through the teaching of history, in which events serve as malleable raw material for the strengthening of national consciousness and the glorification of the Turkish nation, using, as Kedourie put it, 'the past to subvert the present'.[19]

In the teaching of history, the emphasis is on military achievement, with the battlefield as the proving ground of national worth. All the heroes of Turkish history are warriors. Turkish children are taught not only that their history is 'filled with military victories'[20] but that part of being Turkish is 'protecting every grain of the motherland's soil with our lives and our blood.'[21]

The integration of military virtues into the definition of what it means to be Turkish has resulted in the military being viewed as the incarnation of the loftiest national values and embodying the essence of Turkishness. Schoolchildren are told: 'Every Turkish citizen is a willing, fearless soldier in our army which protects the independence and integrity of the country... Our army is the symbol of our national unity and the guarantee of our future, which fulfils its duty to the letter.'[22]

Yet such explicit attempts to inculcate a set of values build on existing social attitudes rather than creating or contradicting them. Most Turks take a genuine pride in their reputation as fearsome warriors. Little boys are told by their parents that: 'Every Turk is born a soldier.'

There is also little doubt that the almost ubiquitous, and often very vociferous, national self-glorification in the education system, the media and even daily conversation overlie a nagging sense of inferiority, particularly when compared with the West; a suspicion that the derogatory racial prejudice with which most Turks believe they are regarded by Westerners, particularly Europeans, may contain an element of truth. The military is the one institution in which they feel they can take a justified pride.[23] Effusive statements by civilians praising the military are often as much about self-reassurance as flattery or nationalist bombast. For example, at the 1999 launch of a book published by his ministry on the Turkish military, the minister of culture, Istemihan Talay, declared: 'The Turkish military is synonymous with the Turkish nation, the institution and the embodiment of the most important values which make us what we are. The Turkish military has given us victories, glory and honour.'[24]

The bond between the military and the public is enhanced rather than strained by military service.[25] For the majority of the population it remains virtually a holy duty and members of the armed forces who are killed while on active service are routinely referred to as 'martyrs'. What opposition there is to military service is mostly concentrated amongst either the urban upper class, for whom it represents a daunting combination of physical hardship and an interruption in their careers, or nationalist Kurds, who balk at the prospect of having to fight against the separatist Kurdistan Workers' Party (PKK).

For most Turkish males, circumcision and military service remain the two rites of passage into manhood. In rural areas many fathers still refuse to allow their daughters to marry a man who has not completed his military service. On the evening before the induction of new conscripts the centres of provincial towns often grind to a halt as young men off to perform their military service celebrate in the streets with their friends and relatives, dancing and singing patriotic songs. Nor, although it may change, is there yet any indication that either the declining birthrate or the casualty rate in the 17 year-old war with the PKK has done anything to diminish such fervour.[26]

The identification of the nation with the military is augmented by celebrations of national holidays, nearly all of which mark military victories and are characterised by military parades and mass neo-militaristic displays in sports stadia with marching cohorts of schoolchildren chanting nationalistic slogans.[27]

The Political Context

Parliamentary democracy is a political ideology which has grown out of a specific cultural and historical context, namely that of the West. It is not a law of nature. Although it is possible to create democratic mechanisms and institutions through legislation, the way in which they function, even in Western democracies, will still reflect the specific context (i.e. cultural values and practices, historical traditions, the security environment etc.) in which they are applied.[28]

Despite more than 50 years of theoretical multi-party democracy, the way in which the political machinery operates in Turkey reflects the values and attitudes of Turkish society, which are authoritarian, patriarchal and conformist rather than democratic and pluralist.

Turkish political culture is built on a system of clientage, a network of personal relations in which loyalty is traded for patronage. It is no coincidence that Suleyman Demirel, in purely electoral terms arguably the most successful politician in modern Turkish history,[29] is known to his supporters as 'Baba' or 'Father'.

Political parties tend to resemble clans rather than institutionalised organisations and form around charismatic individuals rather than ideological conviction or common goals. Advancement within the party is invariably the reward for loyalty to the leader rather than ability. Dissenters are faced with the choice between obscurity and resignation.[30] Under the current political parties law, party leaders are able to appoint not only candidates for general elections but also the delegates to the party congresses which elect the party leaders. The result is a collection of self-perpetuating autocracies and oligarchies rather than democratic institutions.

The premium placed on loyalty has also encouraged political party leaders' tolerance of corruption and nepotism, particularly in the awarding of state contracts, to the point where they are now virtually endemic. Although parliamentary investigations are frequently initiated against politicians, usually by their political opponents, prosecutions for corruption are rare and convictions even rarer; while friends and relatives of politicians have an uncanny knack of becoming suddenly and fabulously wealthy when the politician concerned enters government. It is an indication of the reputation of politicians that during the late 1990s Bulent Ecevit was able to build a dramatic political comeback almost solely on a reputation for personal honesty, culminating in 1999 in his appointment to his sixth term as prime minister at the age of 74.

The low public reputation of politicians has been exacerbated by the failure of successive governments to provide either stability or prosperity. In the absence of a single charismatic leader able to command an electoral majority, over the last 20 years the political spectrum has become increasingly fragmented, as parties with virtually identical policy manifestoes[31] have competed only on the personality of their leaders. This trend has been exacerbated by the strong bias amongst the Turkish public towards right-wing parties and, even amongst ostensibly leftist parties, a virtually universal commitment to an assertive nationalism.

The narrowing of both ideological distinctions and electoral margins (since 1991 no party has won more than 25% of the popular vote[32]) has aggravated an already fractious political environment. There were nine governments, all coalitions, in the period from 1991 to 2000. More damagingly, strained relations within the coalitions as the constituent parties manoeuvre for short-term political advantage, has meant that, particularly over the last decade, governments have lived under the almost constant threat of possible early elections, making it impossible, even if they had the will, for them to pass potentially unpopular though much-needed structural reforms.

The low public regard for politicians, and their manifest failure to generate prosperity or stability, has meant that they invariably feature towards the bottom of surveys of institutions trusted by the Turkish public. In December 1996 only 16.6% of those questioned said that they trusted politicians, falling to 14.4% in January 1998 and then rising to 21.6% in June 1999 before sliding to 15.0% in September 1999[33] following the government's dilatory response to the devastating 17 August 1999 earthquake. In another opinion poll in early 2000, 43% of respondents described politicians as liars, more than twice as many as the next category, journalists, with 19%.[34]

In contrast, the opinion polls demonstrate an overwhelming public faith in the country's armed forces, which consistently top the lists of most trusted institutions. In a December 1996 survey, 81.3% of those questioned said that they trusted the armed forces, compared with 78.8% in January 1997 and 78.9% in June 1999. Even given the collapse in public confidence during the national trauma of the August 1999 earthquake, in September 1999 the armed forces still headed the list of trusted institutions with 65.1%, followed by Turkey's much-maligned police with 51.7%.[35]

Yet, despite the disrepute in which politicians and parliament are held, corruption and nepotism can also provide opportunities. Over 5,000 members of the public visit parliament each day to ask deputies to intervene in issues ranging from the provision of amenities to their village or urban neighbourhood to transfers for relatives working in the civil service or assistance with applications for gun licences.[36]

Public Perceptions of the Security Environment

Popular support for the military is further underpinned by public perceptions of the security environment. Turks are taught, and most believe, that their country is under continual external and internal threat, both from other countries plotting to divide or acquire Turkish territory and from internal forces seeking to change the constitutional status quo. The result is often a virtual siege mentality, riddled with impossibly intricate conspiracy theories.

Public perceptions of foreign threats tend to be based as much on historical experience as current reality. Turkish schoolchildren are taught that the 1920 Treaty of Sèvres, which, though never ratified and subsequently superseded by the 1923 Treaty of Lausanne, foresaw the allocation of large tracts of modern Turkey to Greece, Armenia, Italy and France (the latter two in the form of mandates), and the eventual creation of an independent Kurdish state, still represents the real intentions of the West towards Turkey. As a result, many Turks genuinely believe conspiracy theories in which the US and the EU are trying to weaken Turkey, both through partition (e.g. the creation of a Kurdish state) and through instigating sufficient domestic political turmoil to ensure that the country remains weak and thus easily exploited.

For example, in 1999 at the beginning of a week of celebrations to mark the anniversary of the Turkish victory in the 1915–16 Gallipoli campaign, Ekrem Ozsoy, the governor of the nearby town of Canakkale, accused the former First World War Allies of providing support to the separatist PKK in an attempt to achieve what they had failed to accomplish nearly 80 years earlier. 'Today the same states are using a handful of terrorists as a sub-contractor,' he declared. 'What are they doing? They are giving them mines and rockets.'[37]

Turkish children are explicitly taught to equate territorial with ideological integrity, and to be prepared to defend assaults on the reforms introduced by Ataturk before his death in 1938 with the same vigour with which Turks resisted the Greeks in the war of 1919–22. Textbooks state: 'The War of Liberation and Ataturk's reforms were a whole. The Turkish revolution began in 1919 and was completed in 1938'.[38]

Since the end of the Cold War the two main threats to Kemalist doctrine have come from Kurdish nationalism, initially the PKK although the focus is now shifting towards non-violent organisations, and a resurgent Islamist movement. To its supporters, who still comprise the majority of the population,[39] Kemalism is so closely identified with the state as to be an integral part of it. Those who question Kemalism are routinely characterised as 'traitors', and the mainstream media reinforces the assertion in Turkish textbooks that: 'In our country there are elements which seek to destroy Turkey. The common point of these elements is that they are against the principles of Ataturk.'[40]

Public Perceptions of the Role of the Turkish Military

The combination of social, cultural and historical factors which has exalted the Turkish military as virtually the embodiment of the nation has also endowed it with a security role which extends far beyond that of the armed forces in Westernised parliamentary democracies. Although the Turkish military undoubtedly relishes its role as both guardian of the nation and of Kemalist doctrine, it is not merely self-appointed. It has a popular mandate. Most Turks expect the military not only to protect them against foreign threats but also to intervene to check excesses or restore order from the chaos created by inept and corrupt civilian government;[41] even though the often brusque manner with which the military fulfils its mandate can sometimes antagonise even its most ardent supporters.

Such a mandate is simply anathema to many in the West, where objective analysis is still often sacrificed to ideologically driven wishful thinking. For example, the military-led campaign to topple the Islamist-led government in 1997[42] was characterised by one respected journal as making 'it harder to argue that Turkey was at last settling down to be a real democracy, a place where the people take the decisions'.[43]

Yet not only had the Islamists demonstrated little genuine commitment to democracy but they had come to power with a mere 21.4% of the popular vote.[44] The majority of the population remained vigorously opposed to the Islamists' agenda. In December 1996, in the middle of the Islamist government's 11-month term in office, and as military commanders issued increasingly blunt warnings that they would not tolerate any erosion of secularism, public trust in the armed forces rose to 81.3%, while just 16.8% of those questioned said that they trusted politicians.[45]

It is this lack of confidence in politicians and the political process which, added to the public prestige of the armed forces, has ensured that the public perception of the security role of the military extends into the political arena.

There is a general acknowledgment that: 'When the civilian authorities really begin to fulfil their responsibilities then the military will return to its own field.'[46]

But such a delegation of responsibility to the military to save the nation from the politicians whom the public has itself elected also highlights one of the fundamental differences between the theory and practice of democracy in Turkey; namely, the reluctance of the majority of the public to take the responsibility for change upon themselves. Throughout modern Turkish history rights have been granted by the authorities, rather than won. Although public opinion acts as a constraint on actions of governments, its power is inertial, preventing the taking of unpopular measures rather than forcing the taking of popular ones. Turkey has no history of change as the result of public pressure.

Nor can the public's reluctance to pressure the country's leaders be explained by Turkey's theoretically draconian legislative restrictions on freedom of expression and political pluralism. Such restrictions are erratically and inefficiently enforced[47] and tend to be applied to the margins of the political spectrum, rather than the mainstream. More importantly, they grow out of prevailing social attitudes and practices rather than being imposed upon them. As noted above, Turks do not have a tradition of tolerating pluralism on a social level, most conspicuously in the family, and almost invariably bow to authority rather than challenge it.

Privately, even the military acknowledges that the public failure to take responsibility for change is one of the main factors underpinning its high profile in Turkey. According to one high-ranking officer: 'Once the Turkish people begin to use the democratic system, then we won't want to intervene. Nor would we be able to intervene even if we wanted to.'[48] While the former is debatable, particularly if the mass of the public supported an erosion of Turkey's Kemalist legacy, there is little doubt that the Turkish military could not exercise influence as it does in a truly democratic society.

Ironically, even advocates of a reduced role for the military tend to turn to it in times of crisis. Many former hardline leftists, who had borne the brunt of military pressure following the 1980 coup, supported the 1997 military-led drive to oust the Islamist-led coalition; some in response to a direct approach from the military to unite against a common foe.[49] The Turkish Industrialists' and Businessmen's Association (TUSIAD), which in January 1997 had published a report advocating the reduction of the military's role in Turkish life,[50] was among the most enthusiastic supporters of the military's anti-Islamist campaign. On 4 April 1997, five weeks after the military had effectively delivered an ultimatum to the Islamist-led coalition at the NSC, TUSIAD Chairman Muharrem Kayhan defended the military's action, declaring: 'The NSC has filled a vacuum left by the civilian authorities.'[51]

Yet, widespread public support for the military does not extend to an enthusiasm for military rule. The two occasions when the military has taken over the government of the country are remembered as being oppressive and restrictive, even though the coups that preceded them undoubtedly restored public order. This is particularly true of the most recent period of military rule, 1980–83. In the years leading up to the 12 September 1980 coup, political violence between leftist and rightist extremists escalated into bloody gang warfare, marked by bombings, assassinations and massacres. Turkish society became increasingly politically polarised as leftist and rightist factions appeared even in the police force. By the time the military finally intervened, daily death tolls of 20–30 had become commonplace, and the fear of being caught in a bomb blast or firefight between rival gangs had made many Turks reluctant to leave their homes. The coup was initially welcomed by the public.[52] The military restored order and put an almost immediate end to the political violence; but at a huge cost. Curfews were imposed and public activities forbidden. A wide range of magazines, newspapers, books and films were banned, and the activities of virtually all professional associations and trade unions suspended. Fourteen thousand Turks were stripped of their citizenship and another 650,000 people arrested.[53] Many were soon released, but inter-rogations were often brutal; 171 prisoners are reported to have died as the result of torture.[54]

The military's public mandate is thus for intervention rather than rule. Yet neither does the military have any appetite for long-term involvement in the day-to-day administration of the country. On the contrary, it sees itself as the guardian rather than the ruler of the nation, anxious to remain aloof from what it sees as the pernicious impact of politics on the lofty ideals of the officer corps.

Chapter 2

The Turkish Officer Corps

The Turkish officer corps is unique. It forms an élite within Turkish society, where its high levels of efficiency and motivation, and its emphasis on self-sacrifice and personal integrity are in marked contrast to the inefficiency and corruption that characterise most civilian institutions. However, what singles it out from militaries elsewhere in the world is that it is driven by an indigenous ideology, namely the state creed of Kemalism.

The integration of military virtues into perceptions of the national character has meant that few Turkish officers would disagree with Ataturk's own description of the military as: 'The armoured statement of Turkish unity, Turkish strength and ability and Turkish patriotism.'[1] As a result, the military tends to see itself, rather than the elected politicians, as representing the will of the Turkish nation and having the ultimate responsibility for the preservation of both the nation and the national ideology.

The Structure of the Turkish Armed Forces

The Turkish officer corps comprises an estimated 104,500 personnel,[2] of whom approximately 60,000 serve in the army, 16,000 in the navy and 28,500 in the air force.[3] The Turkish Armed Forces (TAF) are commanded by the Turkish General Staff (TGS), headed by the chief of staff. Although there is no official hierarchy, the chief of staff has traditionally always been a member of the army. Unlike in some other countries, where he is primarily a coordinator between services, the chief of the TGS is overall commander of each of the individual services and is entitled to wear the uniform of the navy and airforce as well as the army.

In peacetime the *gendarmerie*, which is responsible for internal security outside municipal areas, comes under the command of the Ministry of Internal Affairs rather than the TGS. However, it is attached to the TGS for training and special duties, to the army for weaponry and equipment and draws its officer corps from cadets at military academies.[4]

In theory, the TGS is subordinate to the Prime Ministry. In practice, it is autonomous. The Ministry of National Defence (MND) has no authority over the TGS, and its responsibilities are confined to conscription, defence procurement and relations with other ministries. In Turkish protocol the chief of staff ranks ahead of the Minister of National Defence and second only to the prime minister.

The internal organisation of the TGS is similar to the American system of J-Chiefs, comprising seven departments, namely:

- J-1 responsible for personnel;
- J-2 responsible for the collation and evaluation of internal and foreign intelligence from both the Turkish National Intelligence Organisation, the police and *gendarmerie* and the three services' own intelligence branches;
- J-3 responsible for operations, training, planning and exercises;
- J-4 responsible for logistics;
- J-5 is arguably the most important department and is responsible for strategic policies, threat assessment, targeting, budgets and military agreements;
- J-6 responsible for communications and electronics;
- J-7 responsible for studies of military history and strategy.

Recruitment

Each of the services has its own military academy, which cadets normally enter when they are 19-years old for a four-year course. Approximately half of the intake is drawn from Turkey's five male military high schools, which provide secondary education for boys from the age of 14 to 19. The other half is drawn from graduates of civilian schools. Although all three service academies now accept women, their numbers remain very limited. With the exception of the air force, where there are now female pilots, women have yet to rise to prominent positions.

Candidates for both the military high schools and, particularly, the military academies undergo a rigorous selection process, with strict physical and academic requirements. All candidates are also thoroughly vetted, with a particular emphasis on evidence of criminality or political activism. The vetting process covers not only the candidate but also members of his/her immediate family. Until the 1990s the emphasis was on leftist and/or Kurdish separatist sympathies, and political activism by a sibling, or even a cousin, was normally sufficient to block a candidate's entry into the academy.[5] During the 1990s the emphasis shifted towards indications of excessive piety or religious activism. By 1997 officers expelled from the TAF for alleged religious activism claimed that prospective candidates for military academies were being asked to provide family photographs to determine whether either of the parents displayed signs of being devout Muslims, particularly whether the father had a beard or the mother wore a headscarf.[6]

As in Ottoman times,[7] the modern Turkish officer core is drawn primarily from the lower middle classes, particularly from provincial towns. Members of wealthy Turkish families invariably go into business or academia rather than the military, while the limited educational opportunities in rural areas severely limit the intake of cadets from villages.

Although second-, and occasionally third-, generation officers can be found, the majority of officers are first-generation. There is no Turkish military caste.[8] Despite the immense pride that most officers take in their status, many actively discourage their children from pursuing a military career, citing the frequent relocations and uncertain career prospects.[9]

Since the PKK launched its insurgency in 1984, applicants with an ethnic Kurdish background have undergone an even more rigorous vetting. But, as in other branches of the state apparatus, there is no explicit official or unofficial discrimination against ethnic Kurds provided that they act and see themselves as Turks. Similarly, there is no discrimination against members of Turkey's substantial Muslim Alewite minority, provided that they do not attempt to assert a distinct Alewite identity; although a suspicion of central government dating back to Ottoman times means that Alewite families are less likely than Sunnis to encourage their sons to pursue a military career. There do not appear to be any records of successful applications from Turkey's dwindling Christian, primarily Greek and Armenian, or Jewish minorities.[10]

Career Structure

Although there are examples of the use of influence to ensure a relatively easy posting for conscripts performing their military service, in the officer corps itself there are few opportunities for, or examples of, favouritism or nepotism. Most officers take an almost perverse pride in the military's reputation for operating a rigorous and ruthless meritocracy.

Cadets from the military academies graduate with the equivalent of the rank of second lieutenant. In their third year cadets at the army academy are assigned to the various branches/corps of the army (artillery, infantry, armour etc.) according to a computer assessment of their grades and aptitudes. Some of the graduates (e.g. those who have displayed an aptitude for law) are assigned to the *gendarmerie*, where they remain for the rest of their careers. As a result, although *gendarmerie* units may cooperate with army units in, for example, operations against the PKK, the *gendarmerie* remains distinct, both structurally and in terms of personnel, from the regular army.

Once appointed to their first posting, newly graduated army officers can expect to move once every two to three years, with tours of duty generally alternating between developed and less developed regions of the country. The Turkish army is based on a brigade structure, in which armies and brigades remain in a specific location and the personnel move. Command structures within units tend to be highly fluid as individual officers are replaced at regular intervals. It is unusual for officers in a particular unit to serve together in a subsequent posting. As a result, there is little opportunity for the development of cliques loyal to a specific commander or a strong identification with a specific unit or region. Officers are also rotated between different units in the navy and air force, although the smaller numbers of both personnel and possible postings, in terms of airbases, home ports and headquarters, mean that personnel tend to move less frequently than members of the army.

There are upper age limits for each rank and minimum periods of service before an officer becomes eligible for promotion. Ambitious officers can apply to become staff officers after approximately six years of service, at the rank of army/air force captain or naval lieutenant. Each of the three services has its own staff academy in Istanbul. Competition for admission is intense. For example, the army staff academy accepts around 75 officers each year, compared with an annual average of 450–500 graduates from the army academy. However, graduates from the staff academies not only receive extra seniority and slightly higher salaries but are more likely to be offered foreign postings. They also effectively join a fast track for promotion. Almost all of the highest ranks in each of the three services are filled by staff officers. The commanders of the three services and the chief of the General Staff are always staff officers. Staff officers can also expect to spend up to two-thirds of their time in headquarters, compared with an even split between headquarters and the field for non staff officers.

Even though there is little difference in terms of salary, there is a huge gap in prestige between the rank of colonel and general[11] both within the services themselves, where they form an élite within the TGS, and in Turkish society at large, where generals continue to be addressed with the Ottoman honorific of *pasha*. Promotion from colonel to general also represents the tightest bottleneck in an officer's career, with an average of only 24 new generals, equivalent to around 5% of annual graduates from the army academy, being appointed each year.

Promotions are decided at the annual August meeting of the 17-member Supreme Military Council (SMC), comprising the prime minister, defence minister and all 15 four-star generals and admirals. Officers become eligible for promotion to general after seven years as a colonel. It is very rare for a colonel to be promoted to general more than two years after becoming eligible. Unsuccessful candidates can either opt for voluntary retirement or wait to be retired by the SMC, which is usually five years after they become eligible for promotion to general.[12]

In theory, the SMC is chaired by the prime minister with the deputy chief of the General Staff acting as secretary. In practice, it is the military which decides on appointments and promotions after reviewing the relevant officer's file, which covers his entire career, and listening to comments from current and former commanding officers on the council. The criteria for promotion tend to be based on military competence and an officer's disciplinary record. Officers who are deemed to be ideologically suspect are invariably purged before becoming eligible for promotion to general. Discussions are often lengthy. SMC meetings usually last for at least two days. There are strict quotas, with the number of generals decreasing from one-star through to four-stars. Generals normally serve four years at each rank, two in headquarters and two in the field. However, each rank also has its own age limit. As a result, by the time they are appointed general, officers are usually competing against the clock as well as their colleagues. Any delay in promotion, which is often the result of the presence of a relatively young higher-ranking general rather than considerations of competence, is usually sufficient to force otherwise able officers into retirement.

The commanders of the three services are usually drawn from the four-star full generals and admirals on the SMC, who are all ranked in terms of seniority when they are promoted from three-star general/vice admiral. In theory, the chief of the TGS, prime minister and defence minister submit a joint list of nominees for service commanders to the president for approval. In practice, the service commanders are selected according to their seniority by the chief of the TGS, who traditionally informally notifies the prime minister of his choice before the list is prepared for signature. Similarly, in theory the chief of the TGS is chosen by the Council of Ministers, which submits the name of a candidate to the president for ratification. In practice, the candidate is selected by the outgoing chief of the TGS; traditionally the post is filled by whoever is commander of the army when the outgoing chief of the TGS is due to retire.

Government attempts to influence appointments was one of the causes of the military demoralisation that laid the ground for the 1960 coup.[13] The Turkish military has subsequently strongly resisted any political interference at any level of the promotion process. Similarly, any general who is suspected of attempting to curry favour with politicians in order to further his career is likely not only to face ostracism within the TGS but also to be forced into early retirement.

In the last 25 years there have been two attempts by politicians to interfere in high-level military appointments; both of which ultimately backfired. In 1977 the then prime minister Suleyman Demirel attempted to have his own candidate, General Ali Fethi Ersener, appointed army commander prior to becoming chief of the TGS the following year; only for the then president Fahri Koruturk, a retired admiral, to withhold ratification until Ersener became due for retirement, opening the way for the appointment of General Kenan Evren, who in 1980 led the coup which toppled Demirel from power. In 1987 the then prime minister Turgut Ozal succeeded in having his own candidate for chief of the TGS, General Necip Torumtay, appointed over the military's own candidate; only for Torumtay to resign three years later in exasperation at what he saw as Ozal's military adventurism and disrespect for bureaucratic protocol.

Payment and Conditions

The salaries of Turkish officers are adequate rather than generous, slightly higher than those in the civilian service but considerably lower than in the private sector. In late 2000 net monthly salaries ranged from the equivalent of approximately $400 for a lieutenant up to around $1,400 for a four-star general. Serving officers also receive a number of benefits, such as subsidised food and housing, free medical care and access to recreational facilities. On retirement, officers receive a lump sum, which is usually sufficient for a down payment on an apartment, and a pension. Officers and their spouses also continue to receive free medical care until their death.

The social prestige attached to the title of *pasha* means that most generals can look forward to lucrative employment in the private sector on retirement. Those considered to be under threat from terrorist attack also receive subsidised secure accommodation, usually on a military base, and personal protection.

However, those who fail to be promoted to general and retire in their late 40s or early 50s with the rank of colonel often face difficulties not only in coming to terms with the social isolation after 30 years of service life but also in finding alternative employment. Most are forced to take low-paid clerical jobs or to survive on their pensions. The Turkish military currently has no system of counselling or career guidance for officers approaching retirement.

Discipline

Infringements of military regulations are dealt with by military courts, headed by three military judges and with the right to present a defence and appeal a verdict. Military courts are also responsible for criminal acts which are of a military nature and offences that are related to military service or are committed against military personnel or on military premises. These can include the trial of civilians for offences related to the military, such as alleged incitement to avoid performing military service.[14] Defamation of the armed forces, or any other organ of the state, is covered by the Turkish Criminal Code and alleged offenders are tried in civilian courts.[15]

Within the officer corps, discipline is rigorously enforced, particularly in the lower ranks. Provided that it is not excessive, rough treatment or physical disciplining of conscripts by a young officer tends to be overlooked or be punished with a verbal warning from a superior. However, other breaches of regulations usually result in disciplinary proceedings. Convictions for even minor offences, such as the infringement of traffic regulations, can be an impediment to promotion, while more serious breaches of regulations are usually sufficient to ensure that an officer never rises to the rank of general.[16]

Ideological offences are dealt with by the SMC. Between January 1995 and August 2000, a total of 745 serving officers were expelled from the military for ideological reasons, almost all of them for suspected Islamist sympathies. Military officials insist that private religious observance is not, in itself, sufficient grounds for dismissal. They note that even some high-ranking officers pray regularly and fast during the Islamic holy month of *Ramadan*, Turkish infantry still shout the Islamic battle cry of *'Allah, Allah'* when charging,[17] that all Turkish warships carry a Koran and that crews issue the Islamic invocation *'Bismillah'* before firing.[18] Military officials maintain that piety only becomes grounds for dismissal if it interferes with the officer's military duties or if he actively engages in anti-secular activities or propaganda, such as advocating a state based on Islamic *sharia* law.[19] However, they freely admit that the main reason for dealing with ideological cases at the SMC is that, under Article 125 of the Turkish constitution, decisions of the SMC are not subject to appeal. Nor does the accused officer have the right to present a defence. If military officials suspect an officer of Islamist sympathies they initiate an investigation and, if they find sufficient evidence to corroborate their suspicions, a report is then submitted to the SMC. Such investigations are usually confidential. The officer concerned often only becomes aware that he is under suspicion when he learns that a report will be submitted to the SMC. Officers expelled from the armed forces for ideological reasons, usually described in their dismissal papers as 'ill-discipline', lose all rights to pensions and severance pay. They are automatically barred from employment in the public sector and often face considerable difficulties finding a job in the private sector as not only are they unable to provide references but most employers are reluctant to engage someone who has been labelled as an Islamist activist.[20]

Privately, many military officials admit the expulsion procedure is harsh and violates the dismissed officer's basic rights. But they argue that Islamist groups are continually attempting to infiltrate the armed forces[21] and that granting a suspected Islamist the right to present a defence would provide him with a platform to propagate anti-secularist propaganda; while the overturning on appeal of a SMC decision would damage military morale and prevent the removal of what they frequently refer to as 'a cancer' from within their ranks.[22]

Yet, although there is evidence to suggest that Islamists have tried to infiltrate the armed forces,[23] there is little doubt that the military has overreacted. With some exceptions, the expulsions of the late 1990s appear to have been the result of a lowering of the threshold for what is seen as an unacceptable level of piety rather than any increase in Islamist activity in the military. Many of the expelled officers had served for over ten years and not only deny the charges of Islamist activism but insist that there had been no change in their levels of religious observance. They argue that during the 1990s, as the Islamist movement in Turkey gained in electoral support, the criteria for dismissal became increasingly arbitrary and that the mere suspicion of piety, such as their wives wearing an Islamic headscarf, became sufficient grounds for expulsion.[24]

The military also jealously guards the right to penalise its own personnel for other offences and has traditionally vigorously resisted any attempt by the civilian authorities to investigate allegations against serving or retired officers. The pride that officers take in their reputation for personal honesty ensures that corruption and graft, though not unknown, are comparatively rare. The majority of human rights abuses occur in policing situations and tend to be committed by the police, the *gendarmerie* or paramilitary forces attached to the Interior Ministry and known as 'Special Teams', rather than the regular forces.[25] Indeed, during the late 1990s army officers were privately prepared to describe human rights abuses by the Special Teams in the war against the PKK in south-east Turkey as a liability, not least because they alienated the local population and thus impeded intelligence gathering.[26]

However, the TGS invariably refutes, and refuses to cooperate with investigations into, allegations of corruption or human rights abuses involving members of the security forces, especially the *gendarmerie*, apparently because it believes that even an investigation would harm the image of the armed forces. For example, in spring 1997 the TGS refused to allow a parliamentary committee investigating allegations of collaboration between elements in the security apparatus and the Turkish underworld to question members of the *gendarmerie*.[27] Similarly, it has refused to allow external investigations of allegations of the use of beatings, usually by NCOs or lower-ranking officers, to discipline conscripts,[28] insisting that such cases must remain the exclusive prerogative of the military courts.[29]

The Officer Ethos

From the moment that they enter the military academies officer cadets are told that they are joining an élite, which not only embodies the highest virtues of the Turkish nation[30] but is also charged with a sacred mission to protect Kemalism.

The strict military hierarchy starts in the military high schools and academies. Cadets are expected to show deference not only to their teachers but also to students in the years above them.[31] Military officials admit that the hierarchies and deference to authority in Turkish society, particularly within the family, play a significant role in enabling cadets to adapt to a military environment.[32]

Although cadets are allowed home leave and, initially at least, often maintain contact with friends outside the military, the relative social isolation of the academies and the inculcation of a sense of being distinct from society at large inevitably combine to produce an increasing identification with their fellow cadets and the armed forces as an institution.

The academies tend to exacerbate the conformist tendencies in Turkish society. Although cadets are encouraged to show initiative in, for example, solving military problems, divergences of opinion are discouraged, and cadets are imbued with a strong sense of there being a single correct solution to each problem. The same expectations are applied to officers' social lives. Turkish officers are expected to be model citizens, with the implicit assumption that this will include marrying and raising a family; although marriage is seen as preferable rather than obligatory and there are examples of bachelors rising to become generals.

On admission to the academy cadets swear that they 'will eagerly sacrifice my life for my country' [33] and are told that: 'A land is a country if there is someone dying for its sake.' [34] They are also taught to identify patriotism with devotion to Kemalism, particularly the principles of national sovereignty, territorial integrity and secularism. Kemalism's often quasi-religious overtones mean that the cadets' perceptions of their patriotic responsibilities become imbued with an almost mystical intensity.

Military high schools and academies are amongst the most modern and best-equipped educational institutions in Turkey. Students at both military schools and academies study academic and technical subjects, but it is Kemalism which forms the ideological core of the curriculum. Ironically, although the military regime which seized power in 1980 introduced compulsory religious education into civilian education, the only teaching of Islam in the academies is within the context of Ataturk's interpretation of secularism.

Although Kemalism has always been the foundation of the Turkish military's view of the world, it has been taught more vigorously over the last 25 years. In the late 1970s, as street-fighting between Marxists and Turkish ultra-nationalists degenerated into virtual civil war, the Turkish high command decided to intensify the teaching of Kemalism in an attempt to preserve the ideological cohesion of the armed forces. [35] In the late 1980s and 1990s the teaching of Kemalism also became a bulwark against the twin threats from Kurdish separatism and the burgeoning Turkish Islamist movement. As a result, cadets who have graduated from the military academies over the last 20 years are, if anything, even more committed to Kemalism than the officers currently filling the highest echelons in the TGS.

Cadets are encouraged to regard Ataturk as having an almost physical presence in their lives. This sense of immanence is particularly strong in the army academy, where Ataturk was himself a cadet at the turn of the twentieth century. On 13 March, the anniversary of Ataturk enrolling as a cadet, at morning rollcall an officer calls out Ataturk's name and the cadets respond in unison: 'Present!'[36] It is not unusual for cadets to be so overcome with emotion that they weep or even faint when they visit Ataturk's tomb in Ankara or during commemorative ceremonies on 10 November, the anniversary of his death in 1938. Photographs of likenesses of Ataturk's face in the clouds or in the shadows cast by the clouds on a hill are hung on walls in training academies.[37]

Ataturk's Great Speech of October 1927, the *Nutuk*, in which he summarised the Turkish War of Liberation, has a position akin to a sacred book[38] and his pronouncements on a vast range of subjects are cited to support arguments as if they were virtual holy writ.[39]

The Turkish military has an ambivalent attitude towards the Ottoman Empire. It claims to have been founded in 209 BC when the Hun leader Mete Han reportedly formed an organised army.[40] Regardless of its doubtful historicity, such a claim enables the Turkish military to trace its origins back to before either Islam or the Ottoman Empire; and thus disassociate itself from what Ataturk saw as the sclerosis and obscurantism of the empire's final years. The military nevertheless takes a pride in Ottoman military triumphs. Warships are named after Ottoman naval heroes and the TGS headquarters contains a large mural showing Ottomans slaughtering Greek soldiers.[41]

The teaching of history in the military academies places considerable emphasis on the foundation of the Turkish Republic. Cadets are taught that the Ottoman Empire was eroded by a combination of foreign avarice and a paucity of patriots prepared to defend the homeland.[42] They are encouraged to share vicariously in Ataturk's struggle against the Allies at Gallipoli in 1915, his refusal to accept the Allies' attempts to partition the rump of the Ottoman Empire at Sèvres in 1920,[43] his repulse of the invading Greeks during the 1919–22 War of Liberation and his crushing of Islamist and Kurdish revolts in the 1920s. The phrasing is often emotive. Ataturk is referred to as 'the bright sun which tore apart the dark clouds'[44] and 'a soldier turned reformer who demonstrated his genius by sustaining the state that he had established. Now there was a brand new republic on Turkish soil, its borders drawn in blood.'[45]

Such a teaching of history inevitably colours the cadets' perceptions of the present. Continual exhortations to identify with Ataturk and to see him as an immortal guiding presence effectively brings the past into the present. Indeed, cadets are explicitly taught that, although circumstances and methods may change, the external and internal threats to the country – threats which they are legally as well as morally obliged to repulse[46] – are fundamentally the same as in Ataturk's lifetime. For the Turkish officer corps, the resurgence during the late 1980s of the political Islam and Kurdish nationalism, which posed the greatest domestic threats to Ataturk's young republic, is proof of how little things have changed; while international pressure to allow greater political pluralism appears reminiscent of Allied attempts to divide Turkey at Sèvres.

The Military's Perception of its Role

The Turkish military sees itself as the guardian of the Turkish state with a moral and legal[47] obligation to protect 'the Turkish Republic against every kind of threat or danger which might threaten the existence of the state.'[48] It does not differentiate between internal and external threats or between threats to the country's territorial integrity and to the Kemalist principles enshrined in the Turkish constitution.[49]

Yet officers are contemptuous of politics and politicians,[50] and have shown little desire to become permanently involved in the day-to-day machinery of government. Although the Turkish Republic was established by soldiers, Ataturk moved quickly to differentiate between soldiers and politicians in the belief that active involvement in politics would corrupt the military as an institution. In December 1923, less than two months after the proclamation of the republic, he passed a law banning serving soldiers from holding political office[51] and insisted that officers who wished to retain their parliamentary seats should resign their commands. The proportion of former soldiers in parliament fell from 16% in 1923 to less than 4% in 1958.[52] Over the last 40 years only a handful of retired soldiers have attempted to engage in active politics; none with any success. While, with the exception of the MND and the National Security Council General Secretariat, the military has made no attempt to integrate serving officers into the civilian bureaucracy as in, for example, the Indonesian doctrine of *dwisfungi*, or dual function.[53]

The Turkish military's disdain for politics has meant that it has traditionally been a reluctant interventionist,[54] taking action only when it believed that the machinery of government was unable to cope with critical problems[55] or when it feared a deviation from Kemalist principles; and coups have always been seen as temporary, emergency measures preceding an eventual return to civilian rule, rather than attempts to change the system of government and establish permanent military rule.[56] Officers are invariably being sincere when they declare that the military is committed to democracy, not least because it associates democracy with the highest levels of contemporary civilisation; and Ataturk's overriding goal was for Turkey to be ranked amongst the most developed nations. However, the military's conception of democracy is shaped by what it sees as specific conditions in, and threats to, Turkey and is based on its own perception of the expression of the national will rather than just ballot-box results.[57] Such a definition is undoubtedly reinforced by the military's awareness of the high regard in which it is held by the majority of the public;[58] while concepts such as, for example, a state based on Islamic *sharia* law are seen as being *per se* simply incompatible with democracy.[59]

But the Turkish military has learned from experience that, although it can successfully topple a government, none of its interventions to date have been able to install an administration or system capable of ensuring domestic stability or good governance.[60] The military thus now sees outright coups as a last resort to be initiated only when all else has been tried and failed.[61] It prefers to exert influence within the governmental and constitutional framework rather than trying to bring down and replace the government from outside, what it terms as 'fine tuning' the system[62] rather than demolishing and rebuilding it.

The result is a system in which civilian authority is primary rather than supreme. Provided that the civilian government functions effectively and within the parameters defined by the Turkish constitution, the military is content to remain within what it sees as its specific sphere, namely defence, where it is nevertheless effectively autonomous. However, if it considers that the civilian government is failing to safeguard against, or is even actively nurturing, threats to either the country or the nature of the regime, then the military believes it has a legal and moral obligation to intervene. Initially, this intervention tends to be in the form of private or public expressions of concern as the conscience of Turkey's Kemalist legacy. If such statements fail to induce the government to take what the military sees as appropriate measures, and the threat is seen as serious and/or urgent, then the military will take action itself. For the vast majority of the Turkish officer corps, failure to take such action would not only be dereliction of an almost sacred duty but a denial of their *raison d'être*.

A Historical Overview of Military Interventions in Politics

Over the last 50 years the Turkish military has instigated the downfall of four civilian governments, twice (1960 and 1980) through full-blooded coups and twice (1971 and 1997) by applying pressure behind the scenes.

From its foundation in 1923 until the first fully free multi-party elections in 1950, Turkey was ruled by former soldiers who had risen to prominence during the Turkish War of Liberation. Yet the military as an institution remained impoverished and politically quiescent. Officers were actively discouraged from discussing politics and even forbidden from reading newspapers,[63] while many moonlighted by taking second jobs to supplement their meagre salaries.[64] In the late 1940s the army still depended on horses for transportation, and most of its weapons were remnants from the First World War.[65] But the combination of NATO membership and Turkey's first experience of multi-party democracy brought the military back into the forefront of Turkish politics.

Turkey's participation in the Korean War (1950–53), where it sustained the highest per capita casualty rates of any of the US-led UN forces, boosted the military's self-esteem. After Turkey joined NATO in February 1952 Turkish officers, particularly the younger generation, began to travel more widely, to become familiar with new technology and to contrast the equipment and methodologies used by foreign militaries with those used by their own forces.[66] They also contrasted the behaviour of politicians in Western countries with what they saw as the unprincipled and self-serving actions of their own government[67] and were shocked to discover that the Ottoman Empire's former provinces in the Balkans were now more developed than Turkey.[68] Their unease was compounded by the scornful disregard with which the military was treated by Prime Minister Adnan Menderes, a rural landowner whose Democrat Party (DP) took power in 1950 and remained in office until it was ousted by the coup of 1960. Within months of his election, Menderes purged the TGS high command[69] and continued to interfere in appointments and promotions throughout his term in office,[70] while refusing to raise military salaries or improve living conditions.[71] Even more alarmingly for the still staunchly Kemalist military, Menderes appeared less than fully committed to the principle of secularism. During the late 1950s he also became increasingly authoritarian, further suppressing already limited free speech and flouting both the law and the constitution.[72] On 27 May 1960 a group of 37 mostly young officers overthrew the government and announced that the armed forces had taken over the administration of the country. In September 1961, one month before fresh elections signalled the return to civilian rule, Menderes and two of his ministers were convicted of attempting to alter the constitution by force and were hanged.

In the build-up to the 1960 coup the officer corps was deeply fragmented and riddled with rumours of conspiracies to topple the government. Even the clique which finally staged the putsch had no coherent idea of what to do next and split into different factions within months of seizing power.[73] There were also divisions within the rest of the armed forces. For the next three years, different groups of officers continued, often quite blatantly,[74] to plan further coups. After launching failed coup attempts in February 1962 and May 1963, two of the most active conspirators, Colonel Talat Aydemir and Major Fethi Gurcan, were eventually executed in 1964.[75] A total of 1,400 students at military academies were expelled on suspicion of involvement in the May 1963 coup. As a result, there were no graduating classes from the army academy in 1963 or 1964.[76] The experience left a lasting impression on the military. The high command has subsequently given the highest priority both to maintaining internal unity and to ensuring the support of junior officers before attempting interventions.

Despite the confusion and divisions, the 1960 junta nevertheless oversaw the liberalisation of the Turkish constitution.[77] However, neither the execution of Menderes nor a new constitution were sufficient to ensure political stability. After a decade of fractious, mostly short-lived partisan governments and amid mounting political violence, initially by leftist groups but which then triggered a rightist backlash,[78] the military intervened again in early 1971. On 12 March 1971 the TGS issued a memorandum calling for the formation of a new government to restore order and implement reforms 'in a Kemalist spirit',[79] failing which it would 'take direct control of the administration.'[80] The government of then prime minister, Suleyman Demirel immediately resigned. For the next two years Turkey was administered by governments dominated by technocrats and under the watchful eye of the military. Full civilian rule was finally restored by the general elections of October 1973.

As in 1960, the 1971 coup placed a considerable strain on the unity of the armed forces. Nearly 30 years later the extent of the divisions within the officer corps is still unclear. At the time there were widespread rumours of different factions and sub-factions 'one within another and sometimes independent of one another'.[81] There is little doubt that some of the rumours were encouraged by the high command in an attempt to justify its action by claiming that it had forestalled a more extreme intervention by more radical elements in the military. Whatever the truth of the rumours, on 15 March 1971 three generals and eight colonels were dismissed from the armed forces for allegedly conspiring to challenge the 'hierarchical command mechanism'.[82] On 7 July 1971 another eight retired officers were arrested and charged with conspiring against the state and trying to subvert the armed forces.[83]

Yet, like its predecessor, the 1971 coup failed to lay the foundations for either good governance or political stability. During the 1970s a series of short-lived, unstable coalitions failed to control either a growing economic crisis or escalating political violence between leftist and ultra-nationalist extremists which threatened to plunge the country into civil war. The 1970s also witnessed a reawakening of Kurdish nationalism as Marxist Kurds began to form leftist Kurdish parties[84] and the re-emergence of Kemalism's other *bête noire*, political Islam, culminating in a mass rally by the Islamist National Salvation Party in the Anatolian city of Konya on 6 September 1980 which called for the introduction of Islamic *sharia* law.[85] On 12 September 1980 the military seized power, dissolving parliament, declaring a state of emergency and suspending all political parties.

Unlike its predecessors, the 1980 coup was meticulously planned both technically and ideologically, and had clear goals. The high command under chief of staff General Kenan Evren not only succeeded in preventing the factionalism which had characterised the previous coups but also delayed any intervention until there appeared to be no alternative.

In September 1979 Evren commissioned a confidential report to determine the appropriate time for an intervention and the form it should take. On 27 December 1979 Evren expressed the military's concern at the deteriorating security situation in a letter to President Fahri Koruturk and called for the 'rapid implementation of the necessary measures'.[86]

During the next eight months over 1,900 people are estimated to have died in politically motivated killings.[87] The coup in September 1980 put an abrupt end to the bloodshed and was greeted with relief by most of the public.[88] The planned date of the coup was a closely guarded secret. Even officers serving in TGS headquarters in Ankara were only notified one week before it took place.[89]

On 16 September 1980 Evren promised a return to civilian rule 'within a reasonable time'.[90] But the five-man military junta remained in power until November 1983, and the first fully free elections were not held until November 1987. Over the next three years, the military tried to restructure the political system, promulgating a total of 669 new laws in an attempt to prevent a return to the chaos of the previous decade.[91] All the leading politicians of the pre-coup era were banned from politics and their parties closed down.

The junta revised the political parties law and prepared a new constitution which severely limited political pluralism and freedom of expression. It also rewrote the national curriculum and, in an attempt to create an ideological bulwark against communism, made the teaching of Islam compulsory in schools; ironically, and certainly unconsciously, thus helping to fuel the rise in radical Islam which drew the military back into the political arena during the 1990s.

On 7 November 1982 the new constitution received the backing of 91.4% of the Turkish people in a referendum, which also approved the appointment of Evren as president for the next seven years. But the junta received a rebuff in the return to civilian rule during the elections of 6 November 1983. Two days before the polls Evren effectively announced that the military supported the Nationalist Democracy Party (NDP). But the elections were won by the Motherland Party (MP) of Turgut Ozal, with 45.2% of the vote. The NDP finished a distant third with just 23.3%. In a referendum in September 1987 Turks voted, by a razor-thin majority, to lift the ban on the political leaders from the pre-coup era. A little over four years later, after winning the October 1991 elections, Suleyman Demirel was again appointed prime minister at the head of a coalition government.

By the early 1990s the Turkish armed forces appeared politically quiescent, leading several commentators to suggest that the era of military interventions in politics was over.[92] However, the reason for the military's relatively low political profile during the late 1980s and early 1990s was its perception of the security environment rather than a reappraisal of its responsibilities. Its return to a more active political role was a direct response to what it saw as the resurgence of the twin threats of Kurdish nationalism and political Islam.[93]

Even during the late 1980s and early 1990s the Turkish military retained control over what it saw as its own prerogatives, namely defence and security policy. The most striking example comes from the run-up to the launch of *Operation Desert Storm*, when, contrary to suggestions that the military had finally accepted the principle of civilian supremacy,[94] the armed forces effectively vetoed a proposal by the civilian government.

In late 1990 the then president, Turgut Ozal suggested that the military should prepare plans for a cross-border operation into northern Iraq, ostensibly to open a second front in support of the US-led drive out of Saudi Arabia. But privately Ozal hoped that, following what he believed would be Saddam Hussein's rapid and comprehensive defeat, Turkey would be able to take control of the oil-rich northern Iraqi provinces of Kirkuk and Mosul, which had once formed part of the Ottoman Empire.[95] The military vigorously opposed such an operation. Chief of staff General Torumtay was renowned in the military for his painstaking attention to rules and regulations. In addition to his unease at what he saw as Ozal's attempts at military adventurism, he was also becoming increasingly incensed by Ozal's often cavalier attitude to official procedures;[96] in exasperation he tendered his resignation on 6 December 1990. He was succeeded as chief of staff by army commander General Dogan Gures, who simply refused either to formulate a plan for a cross-border operation into northern Iraq or to send a token Turkish contingent to join the US-led allies in Saudi Arabia.[97]

But it was domestic policy that was to bring the military back into the forefront of Turkish politics, initially in response to the escalation in the PKK insurgency but increasingly to combat the rise of political Islam, which culminated in the country's first-ever Islamist-led government in July 1996. However, the military had learned from experience. Although both its goals and its perceptions of its responsibilities remained the same, it changed its methodology, opting for subtle, incremental pressure within the system rather than a full-blooded military intervention from outside. The result was what Turkish commentators refer to as a 'post-modernist coup,'[98] which in June 1997 forced the Islamist-led government from power and created a system in which the military uses formal and informal mechanisms to influence government and to try to ensure that it remains within parameters defined by the military's perceptions of the threat environment.

Chapter 3

How the Turkish Military Influences Policy

The role of the Turkish military in the formulation of policy is based on a combination of statutory obligations and the moral authority derived from its public prestige and record of past interventions. It exercises influence through a mixture of formal and informal mechanisms, both utilising official platforms, such as its participation in the NSC, and setting policy parameters through public and private expressions of opinion. The informal authority of the military as an institution far exceeds that of any politician, including the prime minister, to whom the TGS is notionally subordinate. As a result, its ability to influence policy through expressing an opinion is much greater than any reading of its statutory powers and obligations would suggest.

The military tends to concentrate on security and defence policy and rarely attempts to influence government policy in areas such as, for example, the economy. However, the military's definition of security tends to be much broader than in the West and encompasses not only threats to the country's territory or internal public order, such as terrorism, but also perceived threats to Kemalism.

The military's policy goals are contained in the National Security Policy Document (NSPD), which is usually updated every five years. But the military does not participate in any bodies with legislative powers and is dependent on the civilian authorities for the promulgation of legislation. As a result, it uses its influence to issue what are effectively guidelines in order to ensure either that government policy remains within specific parameters or that the government takes measures to address specific threats. However, occasionally, as in February 1997, the military does present the government with a detailed draft of measures that it expects to be legislated.

But the presentation by the military of specific policy proposals does not mean that they are automatically legislated; nor do civilian governments inevitably immediately implement the military's recommendations on specific issues. There are often delays, not least because of the inertia inherent in the machinery of Turkish government. If the military considers that the issue in question is not urgent or only of secondary importance, it will usually bide its time, and often, but not always, raise it again at a subsequent date. But, if it considers the matter to be urgent or critical, such as a perceived imminent threat to the regime, it will increase pressure on the civilian government to take action.

However, regardless of whether or not the civilian government implements the military's recommendations, it does not subsequently pursue policies or pass legislation which directly contradict those recommendations.

Legal Status and Responsibilities

The three main laws relating to the status and legal responsibilities of the Turkish Armed Forces are:

- The Turkish Constitution (1982)
- The Turkish Armed Forces Internal Service Law (1961)
- The National Security Council Law (1983)

Even though all of the above laws were passed during periods of military rule, the legal definitions of the military's role in Turkey have remained essentially unchanged since 1935, when the armed forces were first specifically charged with responsibility for defending not only the country but also the nature of the regime as defined in the constitution.[1] In terms of legislation, the only innovations have been in the mechanisms through which the military discharges these responsibilities, most notably the creation of the NSC in 1961 and the enhancement of its status in 1983 through a broadening of the definition of security and the addition of the requirement that the Council of Ministers give 'priority consideration' to its opinions. However, as is discussed in more detail below, the importance of the NSC lies not in its legally defined role as a consultative body but as a platform from which the military can exercise its informal authority by presenting the civilian authorities with policy guidelines.

The Turkish Constitution

The preamble to the Turkish constitution of 1982 declares that the constitution has been drawn up in accordance with 'the concept of nationalism outlined and the reforms and principles introduced by the founder of the Republic of Turkey, Ataturk, the immortal leader and the unrivalled hero'[2] and 'affirms the eternal existence of the Turkish nation and motherland and the indivisible unity of the Turkish state'.[3]

The first three articles of the constitution, which define the characteristics of the Turkish republic, are irrevocable and may 'not be amended, nor shall their amendment be proposed'.[4]

Article 1 declares that: 'The Turkish State is a republic.'

Article 2 asserts that: 'The Republic of Turkey is a democratic, secular and social state governed by the rule of law, bearing in mind the concepts of public peace, national solidarity and justice; respecting human rights, loyal to the nationalism of Ataturk, and based on the fundamental tenets set forth in the preamble.'

Article 3 states: 'The Turkish state, with its territory and nation, is an indivisible entity. Its language is Turkish.'

Critics of the Turkish military's involvement in politics rightly note that the 1982 constitution was introduced during a period of military rule. However, the constitutional provisions on the basic character of the Turkish republic predate the 1980 coup. Identical provisions on republicanism and Turkish as the sole language of the state appear in each of Turkey's two previous constitutions, which were promulgated in 1924 and 1961 respectively.[5] The 1924 constitution was amended in November 1928 to include a commitment to secularism,[6] which was subsequently retained in the 1961 and 1982 constitutions, while Article 3 of the 1982 constitution on the indivisibility of the Turkish state, territory and nation, is taken verbatim from the 1961 constitution.[7]

Nor has there been any substantial change in the respective constitutional positions of the chief of staff and the civilian authorities. Article 117 of the 1982 constitution, which closely resembles Articles 40 and 110 of the 1924 and 1961 constitutions respectively,[8] states that the Chief of the General Staff is 'appointed by the President of the Republic on the proposal of the Council of Ministers' and 'responsible to the Prime Minister in the exercise of his duties and powers'.

However, one innovation in the 1982 constitution was the granting to the chief of staff the right,[9] together with the Council of Ministers, to nominate his own candidates for membership of the Higher Education Council (HEC), which oversees education in Turkey, in an apparent attempt to ensure that the curriculum conforms with Kemalist principles. But the final choice of HEC members is still made by the president.

The subordination of the TGS to the MND, rather than to the Prime Ministry as under the current constitution, is often cited as one of the main criteria for civilian control of the military. The Turkish military has traditionally resisted such a change, arguing that, given the way in which the political system operates in Turkey, politicians would then attempt to exercise patronage and interfere in the day to day running of the armed forces.[10]

Yet under the current circumstances, subordinating the military to the MND instead of directly to the prime minister would have little practical impact. The MND is staffed primarily by serving officers on secondment from the General Staff.[11] The ministry undersecretary is traditionally a serving three-star general, and the various departments are headed by serving one- and two-star generals. Perhaps more importantly, given that the informal authority of the military is such that even the prime minister does not challenge it, it is difficult to see how a defence minister could be expected to do so.

Turkish Armed Forces Internal Service Law

The most detailed statement of the legal role and obligations of the military is contained in the Turkish Armed Forces Internal Service Law of January 1961, which specifically charges the military with responsibility for protecting the nature of the Turkish regime, including the Kemalist principles of territorial integrity, secularism and republicanism. Article 35 states:

'The duty of the Turkish Armed Forces is to protect and preserve the Turkish homeland and the Turkish Republic as defined in the constitution.'[12]

As with the 1982 constitution, although the law was promulgated during a period of military rule, most of its provisions are virtually identical to the legislation that preceded it. For example, Article 35 of the current law is identical to Article 34 of the Turkish Armed Forces Internal Service Law of 1935.

The Turkish Armed Forces Internal Service Directive is even more explicit both about the methods that are to be used 'to protect and preserve' and about the military's duty to repel domestic as well as foreign threats. Article 85/1 of the directive states:

'It is the duty of the Turkish Armed Forces to protect the Turkish homeland and the republic, by arms when necessary, against internal and external threats.'[13]

The National Security Council

Under Article 118 of the 1982 constitution the Turkish Armed Forces supply five of the ten members of the NSC, which theoretically serves as an advisory body to the civilian government on security-related issues.

The members of the NSC are the prime minister, the ministers of national defence, internal affairs, and foreign affairs, the chief of the general staff, and the commanders of the army, navy, air force and *gendarmerie*, under the chairmanship of the president.

The president is responsible for setting the agenda 'taking into account the proposals of the Prime Minister and the Chief of the General Staff'.[14] Depending on the subjects on the agenda, other ministers, bureaucrats and government officials may be invited to a NSC meeting. But they normally only remain in the meeting during discussions of a specific subject; and only the ten full members of the council have voting rights.

The NSC was originally established under Article 111 of the 1961 constitution, 'to recommend to the Council of Ministers the necessary basic guidelines regarding the coordination and the taking of decisions related to national security'.[15]

The 1982 constitution retained the previous composition of the NSC. But, under Article 118, obliged the Council of Ministers to 'give priority consideration to the decisions of the National Security

Council concerning the measures that it deems necessary for the preservation of the existence and independence of the State, the integrity and indivisibility of the country and the peace and security of society.'[16]

Article 118 further states that: 'The National Security Council shall submit to the Council of Ministers its views on taking decisions and ensuring necessary coordination with regard to the formulation, establishment, and implementation of the national security policy of the State.'[17]

The National Security Council Law of 1983 defines national security in such broad terms that it could, if necessary, be interpreted as covering almost every policy area. Article 2a states that: 'National security means the defence and protection of the state against every kind of external and internal threat to the constitutional order, national existence, unity, and to all its interests and contractual rights in the international arena including in the political, social, cultural and economic spheres.'[18]

The National Security Council Law also covers the establishment of the National Security Council General Secretariat, which is responsible for collecting information and preparing briefing papers for NSC meetings. The NSC General Secretariat is headed by a general secretary and, in theory, like the TGS, comes under the Prime Ministry.[19] But Article 15 of the National Security Council Law states that the NSC general secretary is always a serving full general or admiral, and in practice the NSC General Secretariat works very closely with the TGS.

The NSC General Secretariat is also responsible for coordinating the preparation of the NSPD, which not only reflects the military's evaluation of the internal and external threats to Turkey but also serves as the foundation of the country's security policies.

The Military's Policy Agenda

The Turkish military only becomes involved in what it perceives as security policy issues. But, as noted above, the definition of security is expansive and includes perceived dangers to both the country and the character of the regime. As a result, national security is seen not just as the defence of Turkey's territory and its political and economic interests, but also the preservation of its Kemalist legacy.

Article 2b of the National Security Council Law defines national security policy as: 'the policy which seeks to ensure national security and the achievement of national goals, covering the fundamental principles of the way in which internal, foreign and defence policy is implemented as determined by the Council of Ministers, taking into consideration the opinions expressed by the National Security Council.'[20]

But the Council of Ministers is not involved in the preparation of the NSPD, which identifies the main threats to national security and sets the guidelines for security policies. The NSPD is drawn up by the TGS, the Ministry of Foreign Affairs (MFA), and the National Intelligence Organisation (NIO) under the coordination of the NSC General Secretariat. Given the military's domination of the NSC General Secretariat, it is effectively the TGS which determines the content of the NSPD.

On completion, the NSPD is presented to the NSC for approval. It is not presented to parliament for ratification. The only members of the civilian government who see the document are those who are members of the NSC.[21] Once it has been approved by the NSC, a decree ratifying the new NSPD, but not indicating its contents, is presented to the Council of Ministers for signature and published in the *Official Gazette*.

The secrecy surrounding the NSPD, and the fact that it is not prepared by the civilian government, have led some commentators to refer to it as a 'secret constitution'.[22] The justification for both the secrecy and the manner in which it is formulated is usually that if the NSPD were drawn up by the government it would, given the political environment in Turkey, not only be constantly changing but would reflect the party-political preferences of the government in power.[23]

The first NSPD was drawn up in 1963. It is normally updated every five years, although it can be amended or supplemented more frequently if necessary.[24] The most recent update took place in early 1997 during the coalition between the Islamist Welfare Party (WP) and the conservative True Path Party (TPP). But the NSPD was not submitted to the Council of Ministers for approval until the second half of 1997, after the WP–TPP had been forced from office and replaced by a tripartite coalition headed by the centre-right MP.[25]

The NSPD is a classified document and, as such, is not open to public inspection. However, the amended NSPD of 1997, which was still in force in January 2001, listed the primary foreign and domestic threats to Turkey as follows:

Foreign Threats
- Greece
- The south (meaning Syria/Iraq)

Domestic Threats
- Fundamentalism
- Separatism
- Organised Crime

The foreign section of the 1997 NSPD warned that there was a strong possibility of a military clash with Greece and that in such a situation some of Turkey's neighbours, particularly Syria, might open a second front.[26] It reiterated Turkey's commitment to eventual full EU membership, although it warned that some EU members were determined to prevent the country's accession.

In 1992 the main foreign threat had still been the Former Soviet Union (FSU). The military admits that in retrospect the removal of the FSU was overdue, although, in an indication of how old habits die hard, FSU uniforms and insignia were still being used for the training of Turkish artillery spotters as late as summer 1998.[27]

The 1992 NSPD had named Kurdish separatism as the primary domestic threat. The new NSPD listed Islamic fundamentalism and Kurdish separatism as equal primary threats and warned that what it described as 'political Islam', namely the Turkish Islamist movement headed by the WP, continued to pose a threat to the country's security.

The 1997 NSPD also stressed what it perceived as a direct link between domestic and foreign threats, particularly in its claims of Syrian moral and material support for the PKK and Iran's alleged provision of finance and training to Turkish Islamist extremists.

The NSPD of 1997 was the first time that organised crime had been listed as a domestic security threat and reflected the rapid growth in the power of the Turkish underworld during the late 1980s and 1990s, particularly the Turkish drug smuggling Mafia, which controls the supply of heroin to Europe.

Following the formulation of the new NSPD in 1997, the TGS also amended its National Military Defence Concept (NMDC), which covers force structure, organisation, personnel, training, logistics, equipment and planning, in accordance with the new evaluation of threats to the country contained in the NSPD.

The 1997 NMDC has been cited as one of the main justifications for excluding civilian government from the formulation of the NSPD. Military officials argue that in 1997 it would have been unrealistic to expect the then Islamist-led coalition government, which denied the existence of an Islamic fundamentalist threat and vigorously courted better relations with Iran, to apply a document which listed fundamentalism as one of the main threats to the country's security.[28]

How the Turkish Military Exercises Influence

The military rarely dictates policy to the civilian government; and then usually only as a last resort when it believes that the situation has become critical. It usually prefers to make recommendations rather than issue directives. In areas in which the military plays an active role in the formulation of policy, these recommendations are often very specific, ranging from precise details of its defence requirements to setting guidelines for foreign policy. In other areas, such as the economy, the military is content to allow the civilian government almost complete freedom, provided that its policies do not threaten Turkey's security.[29]

The methods used by the military to exercise influence vary according to the policy area, the nature of the perceived security threat, its importance or urgency and the response of the civilian authorities. In areas where the military plays a key role in the detailed formulation of policy the military tends to use official platforms, such as the NSC, and informal channels within the state bureaucracy. For ideological issues, or if the civilian authorities fail to respond with sufficient efficiency or alacrity, the military will attempt to galvanise public opinion to apply pressure to the government, issuing expressions of concern either in public speeches or in carefully prepared on- or off-the-record briefings to selected journalists. The high public esteem in which the military is held and its history of interventions are sufficient to ensure that such expressions of concern are usually interpreted as warnings to the civilian authorities.

Institutional Mechanisms

The close links between the TGS and the NSC General Secretariat provide considerable scope for military input into the briefing documents presented by the NSC general secretary to council members. But the military also has its own infrastructure of expertise within the TGS, which is able to conduct research and produce briefing documents, even policy drafts, on a wide variety of issues. Most of this expertise is provided by a system of what are called 'working groups' composed of staff officers.

These working groups are neither recent nor politically motivated, but rather an extension of the system through which the TGS plans and manages special projects: for example, working groups are formed to coordinate plans for military exercises or to prepare training materials. The working groups are not permanent. They are formed and dissolved, renamed and their personnel changed according to circumstances. However, during the 1990s some of the working groups became much more politically oriented. The most important was probably the Western Working Group, which was formed to combat Islamic fundamentalism under the supervision of the Naval High Command. Its duties included monitoring not only violent extremist groups but also the Islamist media, organisations and educational establishments and identifying suspected Islamist sympathisers in the central and local government bureaucracies, trade unions and employers' organisations.[30] Other working groups cover issues such as internal security (e.g. the PKK), Cyprus and Greece, even privatisation and, since the December 1999 EU Helsinki Summit, the EU. The importance given to the security threat from the Turkish Mafia in the NSPD also led to the establishment of an Economics Working Group to investigate, for example, links between Turkish banks, bureaucrats and the underworld.

The main official platform for exerting influence is the NSC. Meetings are usually held once a month at a time and place set by the president in consultation with the NSC members. Meetings can be called more frequently if necessary.[31]

The NSC General Secretariat employs approximately 350 permanent staff, many of whom are serving or retired military personnel, although civilians, mostly bureaucrats transferred from other state bodies, are used to liaise with and collect information from their former institutions. As noted above, the NSC general secretary is always a serving full general or admiral, answerable to, and in frequent communication with, his superiors in the TGS. The working groups in the TGS also liaise with the staff of the NSC General Secretariat.

Prior to NSC meetings the NSC general secretary meets with the president to discuss the agenda. The president may also ask the prime minister or chief of staff for suggestions. Briefings on the topics to be discussed are then prepared by the NSC General Secretariat and distributed to NSC members one or two days in advance. If necessary, these may be supplemented by the distribution of further briefings right up to the meeting and, occasionally, at the meeting itself without the members having time to peruse them beforehand.

In theory, the ten members of the NSC discuss the items on the agenda and vote on recommendations to be made to the Council of Ministers. In practice, the recommendations of the NSC are based on a consensus. The members of the council express their opinions and the president, as chairman, then attempts to formulate a conclusion on which they all agree. If there are objections he tries again. Once consensus has been achieved, the NSC general secretary records the wording of the consensus which is then written up in official format and circulated amongst the members for signature before being forwarded to the Council of Ministers for its 'priority consideration'.

As no voting ever takes place, the numerical composition of the NSC is virtually irrelevant. Nor, during discussions, do the ministers of foreign affairs, defence and the interior tend to contradict the opinions expressed by the prime minister; while the strict military hierarchy means that the force commanders never contradict the chief of staff.[32]

NSC recommendations are thus based on a consensus between three parties; the military, civilian government and president. The military's dominance of the NSC is based not on the number of military members, but on its informal authority and the respect it is accorded by both the civilian government and the president. In theory, the president can decline to bring a proposal by the military on to the NSC's agenda or phrase his summing up of a discussion in such a way that the military would withhold its assent; and without a consensus there would be no recommendation to forward to the Council of Ministers.

Similarly, the civilian government can block any proposal that the military brings to the NSC simply by withholding its assent. For example, in the late 1980s the then prime minister Turgut Ozal refused to discuss a package of measures against Islamic funda-mentalism. The measures were stored in the NSC General Secretariat archive, retrieved and updated to form the basis of the measures presented on 28 February 1997.

But traditionally civilian governments have been reluctant to issue a direct challenge to the military at the NSC. This reticence is not simply the result of the military's record of interventions, the fear of another coup or even the awareness of the military's public prestige. However much some may resent specific statements, deeds or commanders, the vast majority of Turkey's politicians are still products of a social and cultural environment which sees the military as embodying the highest virtues of the nation. In addition to any practical considerations, such as the possibility of a coup or a loss of public support, it is also very difficult psychologically for most Turkish politicians to challenge the authority of the military.

With very rare exceptions, such as during the WP–TPP government of 1996–97, the civilian government does not pursue policies in direct contradiction of NSC recommendations. But neither does it necessarily implement them in full. This is sometimes the result of bureaucratic inertia, but often for fear of short-term political consequences, particularly in an electoral environment where a change of a few percentage points in a party's vote can make the difference between being in or out of government. Yet, although the military often becomes frustrated by government inaction, it remains very much aware that the risks both to the country, in terms of domestic stability and international relations, and to itself, in terms of internal cohesion and public prestige, of a fully-fledged coup are so great that it can only be a last resort. In most cases where the government fails to act on NSC recommendations, the military simply bides its time and raises the issue concerned at subsequent meetings with an urgency which varies in accordance with its perceived importance. However, if the military believes that the situation has become critical then, in addition to raising the issue at NSC meetings, it will also increase the pressure on the government through the use of informal mechanisms.

Informal Mechanisms

In addition to, and often in combination with, institutional mechanisms, the military also uses a variety of informal mechanisms to influence policy. These range from public pronouncements and briefings to journalists to informal contacts with bureaucrats and politicians.

The public pronouncements are usually statements by leading members of the TGS at official occasions attended by the media, such as commemorations, anniversaries or graduation ceremonies at military academies. The strict hierarchy in the military means that, although the statement may have been written by a particular general or his aides, the statements are never personal opinions. The contents, and usually the timing and location of their delivery, have invariably been approved by the TGS. Although such statements occasionally address foreign policy issues, such as the threat of military action against Syria in September 1998,[33] they are usually concerned with domestic issues and targeted at a domestic audience.

Pronouncements of this nature tend to be generalised expressions of concern or commitment, such as the reiteration of the military's determination never to allow any erosion of secularism or the unitary state. Sometimes the statements are responses to what the military sees as dangerous medium-term trends. At other times they may be triggered by specific incidents, such as public speeches by Turkish Islamists. Statements by the military are primarily intended to serve both as warnings to the civilian government and/ or those who pose the specific threat (e.g. Islamists, Kurdish nationalists etc.) and to galvanise those who share the military's agenda, such as Kemalists in the bureaucracy and the public at large, to exert pressure for the appropriate action to be taken.

Occasionally, the military will issue similar warnings in briefings to trusted members of the Turkish press[34] or in statements released by the TGS Press Office. Again, both the issues and the target audience for such briefings tend to be domestic; although the briefing officer, almost invariably the chief of staff if the briefing is on the record, will usually go into more detail about both the perceived threat and what the military sees as the appropriate response than in public speeches.

The publicisation of the military's concerns, whether through speeches or briefings to journalists, does often galvanise members of the government, bureaucracy or judiciary, into action. But it would be a mistake to see such pronouncements by the military as a means of imposing its will on the civilian establishment. Many members of the civilian establishment, particularly the judiciary, are at least as hardline Kemalists as the military and, although they sometimes wait to take their lead from the TGS, they will often act on their own initiative, albeit in the knowledge that, should it be required, their actions would meet with the military's approval.

For example, although chief of staff General Hakki Karadayi privately supported the application to the Constitutional Court for the closure of the Islamist WP Party on the grounds that it would take the Islamist movement a decade to recover from the organisational disruption,[35] the military played no part either in the case being filed or in the WP eventually being closed by the court on 16 January 1998. Similarly, the views expressed by Turkey's chief public prosecutor, Vural Savas in his best-selling book *Militant Democracy Against Fundamentalism and Separatism* are much more extreme in their defence of Kemalism than anything espoused by the military.[36]

Until mid-1999 the military was represented on the judicial panel of the State Security Courts (SSC). The SSCs were established under the 1982 constitution to try crimes against 'the indivisible integrity of the State with its territory and nation, the free democratic order, or against the republic whose characteristics are defined in the constitution, and offences directly involving the internal and external security of the State.'[37] Other crimes remain the responsibility of the criminal courts and administrative courts. Originally, SSC cases were heard by a panel of three judges, comprising two civilians, one of whom served as president of the court, and one military judge. However, on 18 June 1999, during the trial of PKK leader Abdullah Ocalan, the constitution was amended to replace the military member of the panel with a third civilian judge.[38] The aim seems to have been to pre-empt any subsequent foreign claims that Ocalan had not received a fair trial, particularly given previous criticism of the presence of military judges in the SSCs by human rights organisations[39] and the European Court of Human Rights (ECHR),[40] to which Ocalan's lawyers were expected to appeal after his conviction. Although, ironically, historically military judges on the SSCs had usually been more liberal than their civilian counterparts.[41]

Occasionally, if other methods have failed to produce results, the military attempts to influence bureaucrats directly. The TGS is already in regular contact with the MFA.[42] Military personnel in the NSC General Secretariat and MND also serve as conduits for the military's views. For those parts of the bureaucracy with which the TGS is not in regular institutional contact, the military expresses its concerns through informal visits or telephone conversations, either by officers themselves or by trusted intermediaries.

During the 1997 campaign to oust the Islamist-led government, the military also held a series of briefings for the judiciary, press and business community in order to galvanise the country's Kemalist élite. These briefings were reinforced by informal visits and telephone calls to prominent individuals in the bureaucracy, media and business community[43] to ensure their support. The military also applied indirect pressure to secularists in the coalition government, particularly members of the junior partner TPP, who received visits or telephone calls, mostly from civilian Kemalist acquaintances, asking them to consider their positions. The result was a stream of resignations from the TPP, which eroded the coalition's majority and forced the resignation of Islamist Prime Minister Necmettin Erbakan on 18 June 1997.

The ousting of the WP–TPP government was the clearest example of how the military continues to be the ultimate arbiter of political power in Turkey. But it would be a mistake to see the military exercising influence to dictate policy across the board. It only attempts to influence policy in areas which have what it believes to be a security dimension; and its impact, particularly in terms of its ability to initiate policy, is often much more limited than is commonly supposed.

Chapter 4

The Turkish Military's Impact on Policy

The military's impact on policy depends on two variables: the degree to which the military believes that its perception of Turkey's security is at stake; and, if so, the degree of any divergence between the military and the civilian authorities over the direction of policy. However, the military's broad definition of security means that almost any policy area, from education and the environment to defence and foreign policy, can, under specific circumstances, assume a security dimension.

But the military's influence over policy is far from absolute. It needs the cooperation of both the government and the bureaucracy in order to implement policy. It is also aware that an initiative which lacked substantial public support would not only be difficult to apply, but could erode the military's public prestige and thus reduce its ability to influence subsequent policy.

When there is a difference of opinion between the government and the TGS, the military is much more successful at blocking policy initiatives than at persuading the government to be proactive.[1]

The only policy area in which the military does exercise almost total control is defence and defence procurement. In theory, any money spent on defence is subject to strict administrative and parliamentary controls. In practice, the TGS has complete freedom to decide how the funds are spent. When the government presents its budgetary proposals to parliament, defence spending is traditionally the one item which even the opposition does not dare to challenge.

Defence procurement is handled by the domestic and foreign procurement departments in the MND and by the civilian Undersecretariat for Defence Industries (UDI). Procurement is overseen by the Defence Industry Executive Committee (DIEC), which is chaired by the prime minister and also includes the defence minister, the UDI undersecretary and the chief of staff; although in practice the DIEC is dominated by the military.[2] Similarly, the defence minister is theoretically responsible for approving the military's assessment of its procurement needs. In practice, the force commanders submit their requirements to the TGS which formulates proposals, which are then signed by the defence minister and forwarded to the UDI or the procurement departments in the MND.[3]

The domestic and foreign procurement departments in the MND are headed by serving officers, usually one-star generals, while the UDI is headed by a civilian. During the late 1990s the military also began to dominate the UDI, successfully lobbying for the appointment of retired senior generals as deputy undersecretaries.[4] In February 2000, Yalcin Burcak, who had been UDI undersecretary since 1993, was replaced by a physics professor, Dursun Ali Ercan, a retired army captain and classmate of many serving high-ranking officers.

However, in other policy areas the military is usually content not to interfere or try to influence government policy unless it believes that national security is in danger and that the government is not taking appropriate action. Similarly, the degree to which the military applies pressure to the government varies according to the perceived magnitude of the threat, its urgency, the extent to which the civilian authorities appear aware of it and their readiness and ability to respond.

Apart from some of the policy initiatives of the 1996–97 WP–TPP government, which were never applied, over the last 20 years no civilian government has implemented a policy that has directly contradicted the military's recommendations on what the military believes to be a key security issue. But neither does the civilian government necessarily take the action recommended by the military. For example, the right-wing parties in the succession of coalition governments that have ruled Turkey for the last decade have often been reluctant to implement anti-Islamist measures for fear of alienating Islamists amongst their own supporters.

The result is that the military carefully selects the issues on which it will attempt to apply pressure. If a specific issue is not considered to be a major security threat or to be particularly urgent, the military is usually content to notify the civilian authorities of its concerns and merely reiterate these concerns at a later date. However, if the military believes that the perceived threat to national security requires action, and that such action is not being taken, it will apply pressure to the government to take what it sees as the appropriate measures; with the degree of pressure increasing in proportion to the perceived magnitude of the threat and the extent of government inaction.

As a result, the Turkish military has adopted a higher profile on domestic policy issues than in foreign policy. Again with the exception of the 1996–97 WP–TPP coalition, there has traditionally been a cross-party consensus on the general direction of Turkish foreign policy, particularly its pro-Western orientation. The TGS is in regular contact with the MFA, which is often allowed to operate semi-independently of central government. In theory, this enables the TGS to exert considerable informal influence over foreign policy as well as utilising institutions such as the NSC General Secretariat. However, despite occasional minor differences over methodology, in broad terms the TGS and the MFA both share the same foreign policy goals. As a result, Turkish foreign policy has tended to remain within parameters tolerable to the military. Thus, although it would undoubtedly intervene if it believed that there was a risk to its definition of national security, to date the military has not felt the need to attempt to influence foreign policy to the extent that it has tried to intervene in domestic policy, where it believes that Turkey's Kemalist legacy is under severe threat.

Domestic Policy

During the 1990s the military adopted an increasingly high profile in domestic politics in response to the twin threats of Kurdish nationalism and the rise of radical Islam, with the latter, in particular, bringing the military into direct conflict with the civilian authorities.

Radical Islam

The rapid increase in electoral support for the Turkish Islamists during the 1980s and 1990s appears to have been the result of a combination of different factors, comprising both global phenomena, such as the worldwide resurgence in radical Islam and the ideological vacuum left by the collapse of communism, and local factors. The latter include: demographic and social changes, such as rapid urbanisation; higher rates of literacy and exposure to the mass media; the introduction of compulsory religious education into schools by the military junta of 1980–83, which was exacerbated by Turgut Ozal's[5] policy of promoting the employment of Islamists in the government bureaucracy; and the manifest failure of the mainstream political parties to provide a solution to the country's many pressing social and economic problems, such as cripplingly high rates of inflation[6] and unemployment, particularly amongst the young.[7]

Although only a minority of WP supporters were hard-line advocates of *sharia* law, there is little doubt that a significant number favoured a relaxation of the principle of secularism.[8] But the WP did not enjoy a monopoly of the religious vote. Almost all Turkish political parties, particularly on the right, included an Islamist wing. While the vast majority of the Turkish population remained practising Muslims of varying degrees of piety, given the narrow margins between electoral failure and success, no politician could afford to be seen as anti-religious. Even Bulent Ecevit, a committed secularist, declared that 'Islam is the guarantee of our national unity'.[9]

Faced with the risk of alienating potentially electorally vital pious voters by attempting to check the growth in political Islam, civilian governments chose to do nothing;[10] and as Islamist sentiment continued to grew, the electoral incentive to take measures to curb it decreased.

The result was the return of the military to the political arena. In 1986 the then president Kenan Evren had issued a warning to the Higher Education Council, suggesting that it take measures against what he described as the increasing influence of 'reactionary tendencies.'[11] In the late 1980s the then prime minister Turgut Ozal, himself a member of the Islamist *Naksibendi* sect, consistently blocked the military's attempts to bring a package of anti-Islamist measures onto the agenda of the NSC. After the WP won the March 1994 local elections, official speeches by military commanders at commemorations and passing-out ceremonies began to include references to the military's commitment to secularism. After the WP emerged from the December 1995 general elections as the largest party in parliament, albeit with only 21.4% of the vote, the military became more pro-active.

In February 1996 during the religious holiday to mark the end of the Islamic holy month of *Ramadan*, chief of staff General Hakki Karadayi warned caretaker prime minister Tansu Ciller of the TPP against forming a coalition with the WP.[12] Ms Ciller subsequently formed an acrimonious three-month coalition with the MP. However, when this broke down in June 1996, the TPP formed a new coalition with the WP; and WP chairman Necmettin Erbakan became Turkey's first avowedly Islamist prime minister.

During the first six months of the WP–TPP coalition, the military bided its time, continuing to issue statements reaffirming its commitment to secularism while monitoring the government's actions. In this it was helped by the cautious attitude adopted by the WP leadership which, despite occasional inflammatory speeches by party activists, carefully avoided introducing any radical policy initiatives, not least because it knew that it still lacked sufficient electoral support to be able to mount a challenge to the secular establishment.

However, by January 1997 there were signs that the WP was gaining in confidence. Erbakan proposed amending the working hours of government offices to make it easier for civil servants to obey the Islamic proscription on eating during daylight hours in *Ramadan*. On 11 January, during *Ramadan* itself, he even hosted the leaders of Islamic sects, which had been outlawed by Ataturk, to a fast-breaking evening meal in the Prime Ministry. There were also reports that the WP was contemplating allowing appeal to civilian courts for decisions of the SMC, which the military feared could have led to the reinstatement of officers expelled for suspected fundamentalist sympathies.[13]

On 22–24 January 1997 the commanders of the armed forces held a meeting at the naval base at Golcuk on the Marmara Sea at which they discussed what they saw as the beginning of the erosion of secularism and 'a leaning towards fundamentalism, that a certain group was actively promoting and other groups ignoring'.[14]

At the NSC meeting of 28 January 1997, the military called for measures to curb the spread of fundamentalist propaganda. Less than a week later, on 3 February, the TGS served notice that it was prepared to back up its verbal warnings with force when it diverted a column of tanks through the Ankara suburb of Sincan after Bekir Yildiz, the local WP mayor, who had already banned the sale of tobacco and alcohol,[15] made a speech in support of *sharia* law. Civilian Kemalists followed the military's lead. On 6 February Bekir Yildiz was arrested, and eight months later was sentenced to nearly four years in jail.[16] On 7 February Kemalist academics at Istanbul university staged a public protest at which they declared that they would fiercely resist any attempt to introduce anti-secularism into the education system. On 15 February women's groups staged an 'anti-*sharia*' march in Ankara. On 26 February Turkey's leading trade union confederations announced that they were joining forces ready to oppose any attempts to change the regime.[17]

At the NSC meeting of 28 February 1997 the military presented the civilian government with a list of 18 anti-Islamist measures, based on the package rejected by Ozal nearly a decade earlier and ranging from curbs on the Islamist media to the closure of private Koranic schools and courses. Heading the list was a proposal to extend compulsory continuous education from five to eight years. The aim was to shut down the middle school sections of preacher training schools, which the military believed were being used to inculcate anti-secularist values. These schools had grown in number from 398 in 1982 to 467 in 1993[18] and 609 in 1997,[19] when they were turning out an estimated 43,000 graduates a year, far in excess of the demand for Muslim clerics.

The NSC meeting lasted for nine hours. After initially prevaricating,[20] Erbakan finally agreed to sign the NSC declaration[21] proposing that the 18 measures be forwarded to the Council of Ministers. On 14 March 1997 the measures were approved by parliament. But privately WP officials insisted that the party could not afford to implement the measures without alienating its grassroots.[22]

At subsequent NSC meetings the military pointedly asked the civilian government for a progress report on the implementation of the 28 February measures, while increasing its efforts to galvanise Kemalist public opinion. Military officials paid discreet visits to trade union leaders to discuss their possible reaction to a military intervention[23] and even approached former leftist extremists, including some who had been imprisoned and tortured in the wake of the 1980 coup, to ask for their cooperation in combating what they now saw as a common enemy.[24]

On 17 March 1997 Turkey's leading trade union and employer organisations formed what they termed the Civil Initiative Group to lobby the government to implement the 28 February measures. In April and May 1997 the TGS held a series of briefings for the media, judiciary and the business community on the threat to secularism posed by the Islamist movement in general, and the WP in particular, while sources close to the high command informed journalists that a full-blooded coup remained an option of last resort.[25] On 22 May the Public Prosecutor applied to the Constitutional Court for the closure of the WP on the grounds that it was attempting to overthrow the constitution. The WP was eventually closed down on 16 January 1998.

The military also worked assiduously behind the scenes, telephoning civilian critics of the WP to offer support and encouragement[26] and contacting, either directly or via an intermediary, members of the TPP to suggest that, given the threat that the WP posed to secularism, they might care to reconsider their membership of their coalition. On 18 May state minister, Isilay Saygin resigned from the government in the first of a stream of defections that gradually eroded the coalition's majority.

The military also sought to undermine public tolerance of the government by questioning its patriotism. In May 1997 when the TGS launched a cross-border operation to strike at PKK bases in northern Iraq, it informed the press before notifying the government, justifying its action on the grounds that the WP might have leaked the information to the PKK.[27] On 6 June 1997, the day after a highly emotional funeral for 11 soldiers killed when their helicopter was downed by a PKK missile, the TGS accused the government of hampering the military operation in northern Iraq by withholding funds.[28]

The WP–TPP government finally resigned on 18 June. It was replaced by a tripartite coalition between the MP, the Democratic Left Party (DLP) and the Democratic Turkey Party (DTP), which had been formed from former members of the TPP, with MP chairman, Mesut Yilmaz as prime minister.

On 17 August 1997 the new government passed a bill providing for the extension of compulsory education from five to eight years, starting with the new academic year which began the following month. But, although it had achieved its primary goal of toppling the WP-led coalition, the military remained reluctant to entrust the protection of secularism to the civilian authorities, commenting that it was the failure of previous governments to curb the Turkish Islamist movement that had allowed the WP to come to power.[29] Privately, the military was also scathing about all the party political leaders, whom it regarded as self-serving and unprincipled, with chief of staff General Ismail Karadayi describing Yilmaz as merely 'the best of a bad lot'.[30] Over the next 18 months sources close to the military held intermittent secret talks with members of parliament to explore the possibility of establishing an alternative coalition.[31] But the talks failed to produce a result and were finally abandoned in the run up to fresh elections in April 1999.

Soon after taking office the MP–DLP–DTP coalition made it clear that it believed that the military had completed its task by instigating the removal of the WP from power and should withdraw from the political arena. On 10 September 1997 Prime Minister Yilmaz announced that there was no longer any need for the WWG, the department in the TGS responsible for monitoring the Islamist movement, and declared that combating fundamentalism was solely the responsibility of the government.[32] His announcement provoked an angry response from the TGS which not only refused to disband the WWG but continued to submit reports prepared by it to the civilian authorities at the monthly NSC meetings. In briefings to journalists the TGS continued to insist that fundamentalism still posed a grave threat to the country's security.[33]

Relations between Yilmaz and the military remained tense through the winter of 1997–98, escalating into a direct confrontation in March 1998 when Yilmaz again declared that combating fundamentalism was the duty of the civilian authorities. In response, the TGS released a statement warning that: 'Nobody, whatever their position, can make suggestions that will cast doubt, overshadow or weaken the Turkish Armed Forces' struggle against separatism and Islamist activism'.[34] Although privately infuriated,[35] Yilmaz was forced to back down and promise to submit draft bills to parliament for the rest of the 28 February measures.

The retirement of General Karadayi at the end of August 1998 and his replacement as chief of staff by General Huseyin Kivrikoglu triggered speculation that the military would withdraw from the political arena.[36] Although he adopted a lower public profile, Kivrikoglu soon demonstrated that he was just as determined as his predecessor to continue the struggle against fundamentalism. In January 1999 the military academy in Ankara published a booklet calling for a second 'War of Liberation' against Islamic fundamentalism.[37] Over the next two years Kivrikoglu asked for a progress report on the implementation of the 28 February measures at the beginning of each NSC meeting.[38] On 3 February 1999, after a meeting with Kivrikoglu, Bulent Ecevit, who was serving as caretaker prime minister in the run-up to the April 1999 general elections, hastily issued a circular to police and public prosecutors nationwide instructing them to crack down on Islamist organisations and unauthorised Koranic courses.[39]

Ecevit's DLP won the 19 April elections with 22.2% of the vote, ahead of the ultra-nationalist National Action Party (NAP) with 18.0%, the Virtue Party (VP), the successor to the banned WP,[40] with 15.4% and the MP and the TPP with 13.2% and 12.0% respectively. In May 1999 the DLP formed a new tripartite coalition with the NAP and the MP, headed by Ecevit as prime minister.

Many in the military felt vindicated by the election results, particularly the erosion in public support for the Islamists.[41] But the new government proved no more eager than its predecessors to implement the 28 February measures. In July 1999 General Kivrikoglu complained that, after over two years, only four of the 18 measures presented to the NSC in February 1997 had been implemented.[42] On 3 September 1999, in a lengthy briefing to Turkish journalists, General Kivrikoglu nevertheless pledged that the military was determined to continue the struggle against fundamentalism 'for a hundred, a thousand years if necessary'.[43]

The TGS also failed in its attempts to pressure the government into curbing the activities of popular Islamic sect leader Fetullah Gulen, whose combination of moderate piety and nationalism had won him a following estimated at between one and two million.[44] However, the military insists that Gulen is ultimately aiming to create a state based on *sharia* law and that his followers are continually attempting to infiltrate the armed forces.[45]

The WWG has submitted reports on Gulen's alleged anti-secular activities to the NSC and in June 1999 Turkish television broadcast video tapes apparently showing Gulen instructing his followers to infiltrate the civil service and lie low until they were strong enough to try to introduce *sharia* law work.[46] But Gulen's large following has meant that he continues to be vigorously courted by political leaders, including Ecevit.[47]

In February 2000 Ecevit publicly dismissed the military's concerns and announced that Gulen posed no threat to secularism.[48] In August 2000 the Public Prosecutor at the Ankara State Security Court issued a warrant for Gulen's arrest, only for it to be cancelled by the Istanbul State Security Court, prompting General Kivrikoglu to complain that Gulen's supporters had infiltrated the judiciary.[49]

Legal amendments to facilitate a purge of suspected Islamists from the civil bureaucracy had been one of the 18 measures submitted to the NSC on 28 February 1997.[50] In July 1997 the government had even been presented with a list prepared by the WWG of civil servants with alleged Islamist sympathies.[51] But the civilian authorities hesitated, partly for political reasons, (particularly given the absence of any clear threshold beyond which personal piety became a threat to the secular state), and partly because Turkish law makes it very difficult to dismiss civil servants. In summer 2000 the TGS persuaded the government to issue a decree providing for the summary dismissal of civil servants suspected of involvement in anti-secular activities. But in August the decree was vetoed twice by President Ahmet Necdet Sezer, a former member of the Constitutional Court, on the grounds that, under the Turkish constitution, any such legal amendment had to be in the form of a law passed by parliament rather than a decree. Sezer was quick to emphasise that he had no objection to the content of the decree, merely to its form; and he indicated that he would approve a similarly worded law passed by parliament. In late August 2000 the coalition undertook to introduce such a law once parliament returned from its summer recess; a pledge General Kivrikoglu described as 'a test of the government's sincerity'.[52]

Nor has the military been able to rely on the concerted public pressure on the government that played such an important role in the toppling of the WP–TPP coalition. With the exception of hardline elements in the judiciary, especially the chief public prosecutor, Vural Savas who continued to press for the closure of the VP,[53] and organisations such as the Association for Ataturkist Thought, which still staged protest marches,[54] by January 2001 the general feeling amongst most civilian Kemalists was that, particularly after the VP's poor showing in the April 1999 elections, the threat from radical Islam was receding.

On 17 January 2000 during a raid on a safe house in Istanbul, police killed Huseyin Velioglu, the leader of the most violent Turkish Islamist organisation,[55] the *Ilim* Group, usually referred to in Turkish by the generic *Hezbullah* (Party of God), which was alleged to have been responsible for over 2,000 murders, mostly rival Islamists and supporters of the ostensibly Marxist PKK.[56] In a subsequent nation-wide operation, police rolled up the organisation's network and made over 1,000 arrests. The TGS was quick to claim that the often horrifying details that began to emerge of how the *Ilim* Group tortured and executed its victims vindicated the military's campaign against the Islamists.[57] But to the general public, the success of the police operation was further proof that the danger from militant Islam was diminishing.

Yet, although the military-led campaign had fragmented the Islamist movement,[58] in January 2001 there was no sign that religious sentiment was on the wane, leaving a still sizeable Islamist consti-tuency which could potentially unite behind a charismatic leader. Most Turks, from Kemalists through to violent Islamist extremists,[59] agree with the military that the armed forces, rather than the civilian government, are 'the principal obstacle to the creation of a state based on *sharia* law'.[60] If the Islamist movement is able to reunite and once again pose a threat to the regime, there is little doubt that civilian Kemalists will expect the military to safeguard, or at least take the lead in protecting, secularism rather than taking on the responsibility themselves.

Kurdish Nationalism

A similar pattern can be seen in the military's campaign against what it perceives as the other primary threat to Kemalism, namely Kurdish nationalism and the PKK. When the PKK launched its armed campaign for greater autonomy for Turkey's Kurds in 1984 it was seen primarily as a policing problem. However, during the early 1990s, as the scale of fighting in the predominantly Kurdish south-east of the country intensified, the main responsibility for combating it shifted from the forces of the Interior Ministry, namely the *gendarmerie* and the police, to the regular army. The civilian government made little attempt to interfere in the conduct of the war against the PKK, either in terms of strategy and tactics or in pursuing claims of human rights abuses by the security forces, primarily by the *gendarmerie* and the 'Special Teams' attached to the Interior Ministry. Indeed, despite repeated condemnations of 'PKK terrorism' neither the civilian government nor the general public outside the region appeared interested in what was really happening in the south-east. Few politicians made any attempt to visit the region and media coverage was often limited to a few lines buried in the inside pages of newspapers as editors censored or suppressed the reports of even their own staff.[61]

During the early 1990s the PKK had effectively controlled large swathes of south-east Turkey, particularly after dark. In 1993–94 the Turkish military began to regain the initiative, making greater use of helicopters and highly mobile specially-trained commando units within Turkey, and striking at PKK camps and supply depots across the border in northern Iraq. It also sought to deny the PKK potential logistical support inside Turkey by evacuating over 3,000 villages and forcibly displacing an estimated 1.5m people.[62] In late 1994, following the appointment of General Karadayi as chief of staff,[63] the military began a hearts and minds campaign to improve intelligence gathering and undercut local support for the PKK. In 1995 the TGS even distributed a booklet to all soldiers serving in the region with directions on how to win the support of the local populace.[64] It also began distributing leaflets promising PKK militants that they would not be mistreated if they surrendered.

By October 1998, when Turkey threatened to take military action against Syria unless it expelled PKK leader Abdullah Ocalan,[65] the PKK, though far from finished, had been militarily contained. The military had also begun to win the psychological war as PKK casualty figures began to include an increasingly high proportion of prisoners.[66] Declining levels of morale within the organisation were dealt a further, crippling blow by the capture and imprisonment of Ocalan in February 1999. On 2 August 1999 Ocalan announced a cease-fire and called on all PKK units to withdraw from Turkish territory and continue the campaign by political, rather than military, means. In January 2001, although an estimated 5,000 PKK militants remained under arms in camps in the mountains just across Turkey's borders with Iraq and Iran,[67] the organisation appeared deeply divided and, in the short term at least, incapable of conducting an effective insurgency.

The military's first-hand experience of daily life in the impoverished south-east of Turkey soon convinced it that social and economic conditions were fuelling support for the PKK,[68] something which the PKK had long admitted.[69] During the early 1990s the TGS several times suggested that the government should invest in the south-east and create employment.[70] As the military began to gain the upper hand on the battlefield the TGS intensified the pressure.[71] By the end of December 2000 successive governments had announced a total of 17 'development packages' for the south-east. But limited budgetary resources, and the time needed to reap any political benefits, meant that none was ever implemented. In 1998 the military even launched a campaign of its own,[72] planting trees, repairing infrastructure, providing healthcare and organising literacy courses, although its limited scope meant that the campaign served more as a public relations exercise than a genuine contribution to the development of the region.

The TGS refused to become involved in the public debate over whether or not the July 1999 death sentence on Ocalan should be implemented. Although privately the military made no secret of its preference for Ocalan to be hanged,[73] publicly General Kivrikoglu went on the record to insist that the TGS was 'too emotionally involved' for an objective assessment and that the final decision should be made by the civilian government and reflect the overall long-term interests of the country.[74] But the military drew the line at easing restrictions on freedom of speech to allow the expression of a distinct Kurdish identity, which it believed would both fuel support for the PKK and threaten the territorial integrity of the country.

Yet, historically, the TGS has only attempted to exert pressure on the government when it feared that the politicians were preparing to make concessions. For example, although the military undoubtedly approved,[75] it was the civilian establishment, particularly parliament and the judiciary, which drove the crackdown on Kurdish nationalist politicians, which resulted in the closure of the explicitly pro-Kurdish People's Labour Party in July 1993 and its successor, the Democracy Party (DEP) in June 1994. Parliament also needed little prompting from the military to lift the immunity of seven DEP members of parliament, who received substantial jail sentences in December 1994.[76]

But during the late 1990s many Turkish politicians became increasingly aware that a relaxation of the country's often draconian restrictions on freedom of expression was a *sine qua non* for EU membership. Both the signing of the Customs Union Agreement with the EU in March 1995 and, more recently, the EU's decision to include Turkey in the list of official candidates for accession at the Helsinki Summit of 9–10 December 1999, prompted a flurry of promises by Turkish politicians to ease restrictions on the expression of Kurdish identity. For example, in the wake of the Helsinki Summit, foreign minister, Ismail Cem promised an imminent end to the prohibition of broadcasting in Kurdish. Only for General Cumhur Asparuk, general secretary of the NSC, to grant a rare on the record interview to a foreign journalist to rule out both Kurdish-language broadcasting and education in Kurdish on the grounds that it 'could tear apart the mosaic of Turkish society'.[77]

In February 2000 a draft report by the Human Rights Coordination Council at the Prime Ministry included allowing broadcasting and education in Kurdish in a list of changes that needed to be made in order for Turkey to comply with the Copenhagen criteria for EU accession. But the NSC General Secretariat objected on the grounds that such concessions were incompatible with prevailing circumstances and that they would encourage separatism.[78] The provisions allowing broadcasting and education in Kurdish were omitted from the final draft that was published in May 2000.[79]

In December 2000 a TGS report[80] insisted that the PKK remained a threat to Turkey's territorial integrity and that it was using the issue of broadcasting and education in Kurdish as a stepping stone towards its ultimate goal of establishing an independent Kurdish state.[81] Embarrassingly, and no doubt knowingly, the report was shown to selected journalists at the same time as Ecevit was attending the EU summit in Nice, where he was expected to come under intense pressure to relax restrictions on the use of the Kurdish language.[82]

In recent years the military has also influenced issues on the periphery of its definition of security, such as the date of the 1999 general elections and the selection of a suitable candidate for president in spring 2000. But on each occasion its impact was preventative, rather than initiatory.

For example, in March 1999 there was considerable speculation in the Turkish media, led by President Suleyman Demirel, about a possible postponement of the general elections which were due to be held on 18 April. The air of uncertainty triggered a bear run on the Istanbul Stock Exchange. However, on the evening of 17 March General Kivrikoglu told Turkish television that 'the postponement of the elections could lead to chaos'.[83] The following day, in an indication of where investors believed the real power in Turkey lay, stock prices surged by 3.8%,[84] the speculation in the media disappeared, and the elections were held on schedule. Yet, although they were reassured, military officials nevertheless insisted that if the civilian authorities had decided to postpone the elections the TGS would have been powerless to prevent them, noting that it would have been ludicrous even to contemplate a resort to armed force under such circumstances.[85]

In April 2000 as the ruling coalition debated possible nominees to succeed President Demirel when his seven-year term expired the following month,[86] General Kivrikoglu announced that the successful candidate should be 'honest, serious and untainted'.[87] Privately, sources close to the military admitted that, in addition to specifying general qualities, General Kivrikoglu was also anxious to debar Mesut Yilmaz, who was known to harbour presidential ambitions[88] but who had clashed repeatedly with the TGS during his term as prime minister and whom the military suspected of being corrupt.[89] On 15 April General Kivrikoglu paid an unscheduled visit to Prime Minister Ecevit to relay the military's concerns, although he did not suggest any candidates of his own.[90] Mesut Yilmaz did not stand as a candidate. On 25 April the coalition nominated a constitutional judge, Ahmet Necdet Sezer. Ecevit proudly announced that the media had learned of the government's choice before the military.[91]

Yet in areas where the military does not perceive a current or potential security threat it has been prepared to allow the civilian government almost complete freedom of action. For example, although working groups in the TGS monitor the economy and have prepared briefings for the high command on issues such as privatisation and the banking sector, its conclusions and policy recommendations have been virtually identical to those of the policy units of the Turkish Treasury, Central Bank and State Planning Organisation; with the result that to date the military has not made any serious attempt to influence economic policy.

Foreign Policy

The overall orientation of Turkish foreign policy has remained unchanged since the 1920s when Ataturk identified becoming a modern, Westernised, European state as an ideal to which Turkey should aspire. Today most Turks regard EU membership as the criterion for being truly European. Accession means more than mere economic or political benefits. It is a question of identity, of being able to number themselves amongst what they perceived as the élite of nations; which is why criticism by, and continued exclusion from, the EU often triggers such emotional reactions inside Turkey.

But the broad cross-party consensus on the general direction of foreign policy has also meant that it is seen as state policy, which governments serve rather than dictate. Consequently, as the state institution primarily responsible, the MFA has developed considerable de facto autonomy in the day-to-day conduct of foreign policy. While the NSC sets general strategic parameters for foreign policy and usually assumes direct responsibility for its implementation in security sensitive areas such as Cyprus or the PKK.

MFA personnel are drawn from a handful of university faculties and tend to be not only the best educated but also the most ideologically homogenous component of the civilian bureaucracy: nationalistic, Kemalist, pro-NATO and pro-EU membership.[92] The MFA's perceptions of Turkey's national interests differ little from those of the military, although there are sometimes divergences of opinion over how best they should be pursued: for example, during the mid-1990s the TGS was often frustrated by the MFA's reluctance to adopt a harder line against countries suspected of supporting the PKK.[93]

MFA personnel work closely with their counterparts in the TGS, both exchanging information and cooperating in the preparation of briefing documents for their respective superiors and for presentation to the NSC. In areas with a significant security component, MFA desk officers are often in daily contact with their counterparts in the TGS, either in face-to-face meetings or by telephone.[94] Any differences are usually resolved before briefing documents or policy drafts are completed. But such differences tend to be rare and minor; with the result that the TGS usually simply does not need to try to apply pressure to change foreign policy.

For example, in 1999 working groups within the TGS produced a report on the utilisation of transboundary water resources, focussing on the Tigris and Euphrates, whose water flow is controlled by Turkish dams. The report confirmed the findings of other Turkish institutions, rejecting claims by Damascus and Baghdad that Turkey was not allowing enough water to flow downstream and that any shortages were the result of inefficient practices in Syria and Iraq.[95] Similarly, the TGS has joined with the MFA and other governmental institutions in arguing for the construction of a pipeline to carry Caspian Sea oil from the Azeri capital of Baku to Ceyhan on the Turkish Mediterranean coast.

Syria

However, the 1998 campaign to force Syria to expel PKK leader Abdullah Ocalan demonstrated both how the TGS can take the initiative in foreign policy and how it cooperates with other elements in the state apparatus. In July 1997 the TGS backed a decision by the new MP–DLP–DP coalition to resume its dialogue with Damascus in an attempt to persuade Syria to withdraw its support for the PKK. But high-level meetings between Syrian and Turkish diplomats in February and July 1998 failed to produce any concrete results.

Meanwhile, the TGS had formulated a plan for what it called 'controlled crisis management', in which the military and the MFA would attempt to increase pressure on Syria until it expelled Ocalan.[96] The plan was approved at the NSC meeting of August 1998. Not only was the decision taken at the NSC rather than the Council of Ministers, but it was the military, rather than the civilian authorities, which took the initiative. On 16 September 1998, during a visit to a command post on the border with Syria, First Army Commander General Atilla Ates bluntly warned Damascus that: 'Our patience is exhausted. If the necessary measures are not taken, we as the Turkish nation will be forced to take every kind of measure.'[97]

Three days later the chief of staff, General Huseyin Kivrikoglu repeated the warning at a speech in the south-eastern city of Adana.

The military began a massive build-up of troops and armour along the Syrian border, while Turkish fighter planes practised sorties along the boundaries of Syrian airspace.[98] On 1 October at the opening of the new session of parliament, President Demirel declared that Turkey would no longer tolerate Syrian support for the PKK. On the following day Prime Minister Mesut Yilmaz told journalists that the Turkish forces were awaiting orders to launch an assault.[99] Military officials remain adamant that, if Damascus had not backed down, they would have launched a cross-border operation against PKK camps in Syria, albeit along the lines of attacks on PKK bases in northern Iraq rather than a full-scale invasion.[100]

On 9 October 1998, after shuttle diplomacy by Egyptian President Hosni Mubarak convinced Syria that Turkey was serious, Ocalan was finally expelled from Damascus. On 10 October Turkish and Syrian officials signed an agreement in Adana under which Damascus undertook to prevent Ocalan's return and prohibit 'all activities of the PKK and its affiliated organisations on its territory'.[101]

Iran

But the military has been less successful in initiating action against Iran, which it accuses of supporting violent Turkish Islamist groups and tolerating PKK bases in the mountains along its border with Turkey. One of the 18 proposals presented to the NSC by the military on 28 February 1997 called for the 'preparation and implementation of measures against Iran to prevent its destructive and damaging activities without disrupting economic or neighbourly relations.'[102] But no measures were taken.

By 2000 the military had shifted its attention to the presence of groups of PKK militants in Iran. On 27 June 2000 General Atilla Ates, now land forces commander, issued a strongly worded warning to Teheran to close the PKK bases,[103] while privately sources close to the TGS insisted that the military was prepared to launch air strikes against PKK positions on Iranian territory.[104] Yet, although the military's ability to set parameters for relations at the NSC continues to preclude closer ties with Teheran, by January 2001 neither had any concrete measures been taken against Iran. The main reason appeared to be an awareness, by both the TGS and the civilian authorities, that the military stakes were much higher than during the confrontation with Syria in 1998. In addition, despite the wording of the clause in the proposals of 28 February 1997, almost any action taken against Teheran would inevitably have a negative impact on bilateral economic relations; while Iran also controls the land routes linking Turkey with Central Asia.

Iraq

It is also the NSC, rather than the Council of Ministers, which oversees Turkey's policy towards Iraq, particularly northern Iraq. There has always been considerable public opposition in Turkey both to UN sanctions against Baghdad[105] and to *Operation Northern Watch*, under which US/UK air patrols flying out of the Incirlik airbase in south-east Turkey enforce the no-fly zone over northern Iraq. But, despite frequent threats by civilian politicians to abolish *Northern Watch*, the NSC has consistently recommended the renewal of its mandate; and parliament has always followed its recommendations.

The NSC has also closely controlled cross-border trade between south-eastern Turkey and northern Iraq, tolerating a limited volume in an attempt to boost the local economy, without allowing a flagrant abrogation of sanctions. But the NSC's recommendations concerning northern Iraq reflect state policy rather the impositions of the military. For example, although both the TGS and the MFA strongly oppose the de facto creation of an albeit fractured Kurdish state in northern Iraq, neither wishes to antagonise Turkey's NATO allies by refusing to renew *Northern Watch*'s mandate. While, as long as the safe haven in northern Iraq exists, it is undoubtedly easier for the TGS to strike at PKK camps there without fear of interference from Iraqi planes. Similarly, neither the MFA nor the TGS is anxious to incur international opprobrium by breaking UN sanctions.

Israel

It was the TGS which took the initiative by forging closer ties with Israel during the late 1990s. But, as with Turkish policy towards Iraq, opposition has come more from the general public than other state institutions. MFA officials make little secret that they believe the warming in Turco-Israeli relations was both natural and overdue.[106]

It was the Turkish military rather than the civilian government which was the driving force behind the signing of the

Military Training and Cooperation Agreement between Turkey and Israel in February 1996.[107] The agreement enabled Israel to train in Turkey's extensive territory and airspace, while Turkish pilots gained access to Israeli training facilities, and Turkish and Israeli naval forces participated in joint search-and-rescue exercises in the Mediterranean. In addition, Israel was able to provide Turkey with satellite and human intelligence, including information on PKK activities and bases in Syria. Between 1997 and 1999 Israeli firms were also awarded a string of lucrative defence contracts.

Yet, despite the fears of the Arab states, the 1996 agreement with Israel has produced neither an abandonment of Turkish state policy of recognising the Palestinians' right to statehood[108] nor a strategic alliance. Significantly, during Turkey's confrontation with Syria in autumn 1998, Israel restricted military activity along its border with Syria and repeatedly assured Damascus that it would play no part, either directly or indirectly, in any possible conflict.

Privately, Turkish military officials admit that they had hoped that the 1996 agreement would have enabled them to access US technology through Israel,[109] noting that US defence sales to Turkey had often run into opposition in Congress. However, although the US welcomed closer Turkish–Israeli ties, it refused to relax restrictions on technology transfers and declined to involve Turkey in the joint US–Israeli *Arrow*-2 anti-tactical ballistic missile system.

By January 2001, although representatives of both the MFA and the TGS continued to hold regular meetings with their Israeli counterparts, there were signs that the relationship between the two countries had lost momentum. Israeli firms began to lose out to competitors from other countries in Turkish defence contracts. In summer 2000, amid press reports of pressure from other countries,[110] two contracts worth a total of $624m were put back out to tender after having apparently been awarded to Israeli companies.[111]

Closer ties with Israel are also constrained by public opinion. The enthusiasm for closer relations with Israel amongst the Turkish élite, particularly in the MFA and the TGS, is not shared by the general public. Although there is widespread social prejudice in Turkey against Arabs, in any confrontation between Palestinians and Israelis – such as the renewal of the Palestinian *intifada* in October 2000 – racism is invariably overridden by a sense of Muslim solidarity, tinged with a nationalist nostalgia for Ottoman leadership of the Islamic world. Such sentiments act as a potential constraint not only on civilian governments, who are dependent on electoral support, but also on the Turkish military, which remains dependent on public support. Thus, although the military is prepared to strengthen relations with Israel in specific areas – such as cooperation against a perceived impending missile threat from Turkey's neighbours[112] – it not only has no plans to form a strategic alliance with Israel,[113] but under current circumstances it would be prevented from doing so by public opinion.[114]

In April 2000 Turco-Israeli relations suffered a major setback when the Israeli Education Minister Yossi Sarid and Justice Minister Yossi Beilin described the 1915 killings and deportations of Armenians during the final years of the Ottoman Empire as a genocide.[115] The allegations of genocide have always been vehemently denied by Turkey. Although the Israeli government was quick to reassure Ankara that the ministers were merely expressing their personal opinions, their statements have nevertheless severely damaged Turkish confidence in Israel.

The seriousness with which the TGS takes such allegations was demonstrated on 4 October 2000 when chief of staff, General Kivrikoglu cancelled a planned visit to Washington the day after the House of Representatives International Relations Committee passed a non-binding resolution recognising Armenian claims of a genocide in 1915.[116]

The US and NATO

General Kivrikoglu's decision also highlighted the Turkish military's often ambivalent attitude towards the US. The TGS respects US military might, but remains suspicious of its motives. The Johnson Letter of 1964, which bluntly instructed Turkey not to intervene in Cyprus, and the arms embargo that followed the 1974 Turkish invasion of the island, are deeply ingrained in the TGS' institutional memory.[117]

Many in the TGS also suspect that the US, along with other Western powers, favours the establishment of an independent Kurdish state in northern Iraq which would eventually lay claim to Turkish territory.[118] However bizarre such a view may appear in Washington, neither is the military immune to a widely held Turkish suspicion that the US actively encourages a measure of internal instability in Turkey and that pressure for the lifting of restrictions on the expression of an explicitly Kurdish or Islamist identity are ultimately intended to foment domestic turmoil and ensure that the country remains weak and pliable.[119]

Nevertheless, the TGS regards the US as a less critical ally than the EU, particularly over issues such as the military's cross-border raids against PKK bases in northern Iraq. The TGS also attaches considerable importance to its membership of NATO, which it acknowledges as having played a key role in the modernisation of the Turkish military[120] and whose members – particularly the US – supply most of its defence procurement needs. Occasionally, the importance given to NATO has resulted in a divergence of opinion between the TGS and the MFA, although the difference has tended to be of degree or emphasis rather than the direction of policy.

However, on issues such as the European Strategic Defence Identity (ESDI) and the European Strategic Defence Project (ESDP), the MFA, TGS and civilian government have been unanimous in arguing for Turkish participation in the decision-making processes with no discernible differences between them.

Greece and Cyprus

During the mid-1990s the Turkish military did become increasingly concerned by the possibility of a deviation from state policy towards Greece and Cyprus. But the concerns were triggered by the civilian government rather than the MFA, whose views have remained virtually identical to those of the TGS. In early 1995 the then prime minister, Tansu Ciller appeared willing to make concessions over Cyprus in order to secure a Customs Union agreement with the EU.[121] In January 1996 the TGS was further alarmed by Ciller's naivety and adventurism when Turkey and Greece came to the brink of war over the disputed Aegean islet of Imia/Kardak. During an emergency meeting to discuss a Greek landing on the islet, Ciller first asked whether it belonged to Turkey and, after being told that it did, proposed sending in troops and expelling the Greeks by force. She was informed by the head of the navy, Admiral Guven Erkaya, that such an operation would be tantamount to a declaration of war against Greece and was persuaded to land Turkish commandos on a nearby islet whose sovereignty was not in dispute.[122] The stand-off was finally resolved when Athens was persuaded to withdraw its troops under pressure from Washington. But the TGS subsequently ensured that all policy concerning Cyprus and Greece was controlled by the NSC.[123]

The apparent rapprochement between Turkey and Greece following the earthquakes in the two countries in 1999 has done little to persuade the military to relax its vigilance. In January 2001 neither the military nor officials in the MFA shared Turkish foreign minister Ismail Cem's conviction that his ongoing dialogue with Greek foreign minister Giorgos Papandreou had produced anything of substance. The TGS noted that the two ministers had yet to agree on the nature of their countries' differences, much less discuss possible solutions. Greece insists that the only problem is the definition of the continental shelf, while Turkey maintains that they also need to resolve differences over mineral exploration rights, airspace, Greece's right to extend its territorial waters and the ownership of a number of Aegean islets.

The extent to which the military still dominates policy towards Greece was clearly demonstrated in May 2000. On his retirement from active service in 1997, Admiral Erkaya was appointed as an adviser to the Prime Ministry. In May 2000 Erkaya prepared a report which recommended the abolition of the Turkish Third Army. The Third Army is based in the Aegean region of Turkey and comprises a total of 100,000 troops in six brigades. It was created in the aftermath of the 1974 Turkish invasion of Cyprus. Turkey insists that its main functions are training and defence against a possible attack from Greece. Athens maintains that it has an offensive capability, with Greece as its target. On 22 May 2000 Turkish government officials indicated that they would consider Erkaya's recommendation.[124] On the following day the TGS released a statement saying that any change to the status of the Third Army was 'not on the agenda'.[125] The proposal has not been discussed again.

The TGS plays an even more proactive role in policy on Cyprus, both through the NSC and through its military presence in the north of the island. The TGS is committed to Turkish state policy, shared by both the MFA and politicians, of a confederal solution to the Cyprus problem, which they argue is the only guarantee of Turkish Cypriots' safety. But privately military officials also cite strategic considerations and are adamant that Turkey could never again permit a potentially hostile state – which they believe a unified Cyprus dominated by Greek Cypriots would be – so close to its southern coast.[126]

In addition to the 30,000 Turkish troops stationed within the borders of the self-proclaimed Turkish Republic of Northern Cyprus (TRNC), the TGS also effectively controls the Turkish Cypriot security forces, which are commanded by a serving Turkish one-star general who reports to TRNC president Rauf Denktash; thus providing a regular, direct channel of communication between Denktash and the TGS. In June 2000 the TGS used the commander of the Turkish Cypriot security forces, General Ali Nihat Ozeyranli, to intervene directly in Turkish Cypriot internal politics.

Most Turkish Cypriots are genuinely grateful to Turkey for its military intervention in 1974, which they believe saved them from ethnic cleansing by the Greek Cypriots. However, during the late 1990s many became increasingly uneasy at the way in which a distinctive Turkish Cypriot identity was being eroded by settlers from mainland Turkey, who by the end of decade accounted for approximately half of the TRNC's population.[127] There was also considerable resentment at the way in which, without any mandate from the Turkish Cypriot public, both Denktash and Ankara consistently threatened to integrate the TRNC into Turkey if the Greek Cypriots were granted EU membership. In fact, in August 2000 opinion polls reported that only 7.7% of Turkish Cypriots supported integration.[128] Against this background, in spring 2000 the Communal Liberation Party (CLP), the junior partner in the coalition government headed by Denktash's arch-rival Prime Minister Dervis Eroglu, proposed amending Article 10 of the TRNC's constitution to transfer authority over the police and fire brigade from the Turkish Cypriot security forces – which had meant that they were under the command of a Turkish general – to the Interior Ministry. On 29 June General Ozeyranli publicly described the proposed constitutional amendment as 'an act of treason',[129] implied that CLP Chairman Mustafa Akinci was a traitor and subsequently had the editor of a newspaper[130] which supported the amendment arrested on apparently unsubstantiated charges of spying for the Greek Cypriots.[131] In January 2001 the constitutional amendment had still not been brought before the TRNC parliament and there appeared little likelihood of it being debated in the foreseeable future.

Given the strict hierarchy in the Turkish military, it is unthinkable for a one-star general to make such statements without approval from his superiors. While there is no indication to suggest that either the MFA or the civilian government disagreed with the content of General Ozeyranli's speech, neither appear to have been consulted by the TGS beforehand.

The TGS also dominates security policy regarding Cyprus, although again there is no indication of any opposition from either the MFA or the civilian government. For example, in January 1997 when the Greek Cypriots announced plans to deploy Russian surface-to-air S-300 missiles in the south of the island, Turkey threatened to use force if necessary to prevent their installation. Although both the MFA and the government were adamant that the missiles could never be deployed,[132] privately TGS officials insisted that they – i.e. the military – would destroy the S-300s regardless of the opinions of the civilian authorities in Ankara.[133] It was also the TGS which decided to include the destruction of replicas of S-300s in highly publicised military exercises in the TRNC in November 1997,[134] and it was General Kivrikoglu, then commander of the land forces, rather than a civilian politician, who, in a reference to the events preceding the 1974 invasion, told journalists watching the exercise: 'Let that be a warning to those who did not pay attention last time.'[135]

Similarly, in June 1998[136] the decision to send Turkish F-16 fighter bombers to the TRNC in response to the landing of Greek F-16s at the Greek Cypriot airbase in Paphos was taken by the TGS, not the civilian government in Ankara.[137]

The EU

The military has adopted a more ambivalent attitude towards EU membership. Turkey was offered official candidate status at the EU summit in Helsinki on 9–10 December 1999. But the wording of the EU offer effectively made Turkish accession conditional on the resolution of all of its disputes with Greece, either bilaterally by 2004 or, if this proved impossible, by allowing them to be settled by the International Court of Justice at the Hague; something which Ankara had previously refused to do. The Turkish government hesitated before accepting. Yet the doubts came from within the Council of

Ministers and the MFA,[138] rather than the TGS, which made little effort to influence the decision.

In early 2000 the TGS established a Working Group on EU membership. But it soon made it clear that it had reservations not about the principle of EU membership – which it sees as the realisation of Ataturk's dream of Turkey being accepted as a modern, European state[139] – but rather the possible impact of the fulfilment of the Copenhagen criteria on the nature of the Turkish regime.

Military officials acknowledge that Turkey needs to improve its human rights record[140] and the TGS has made it clear that it would not oppose the abolition of capital punishment.[141] Chief of staff General Kivrikoglu has even publicly indicated the military's willingness to amend the numerical balance of the NSC in favour of the civilians;[142] although in practice, given that the NSC never votes on issues, the military's informal authority would ensure that it was still able to dominate proceedings.

The military's main fear is that the relaxation of Turkey's often draconian restrictions on freedom of speech would fuel anti-secular and separatist, primarily Kurdish nationalist, sentiments. In June 2000 the NSC declared that it would monitor all constitutional, legal and administrative amendments related to the EU.[143] Military officials argue that no other European country faces the same threats as Turkey and that the Copenhagen criteria should be implemented 'taking into consideration the interests and realities of the country'.[144] On 9 October 2000, deputy chief of staff General Yasar Buyukanit declared that: 'Entering the EU is a prerequisite for the realisation of the goal of modernisation laid down by Ataturk. But it is Turkey's most natural right to take the measures necessary to preserve its unitary and secular structure in pursuit of such a goal'.[145]

Yet there is little doubt that the military's concerns are shared by many bureaucrats, including members of the MFA, and civilian politicians, particularly on the nationalist right. (Ironically, the Helsinki offer of candidacy took place under the most explicitly nationalist government in Turkey's post-war history.) Significantly, despite Prime Minister Ecevit's declaration after the Helsinki Summit that Turkey would fulfil all the requirements for accession by the end of 2002, by January 2001 nothing had been done, even in those areas, such as the abolition of capital punishment, where the military had already indicated that it had no objections.

Conclusion

The role of the military in Turkey is the result of a combination of context and circumstance, a symptom rather than a cause of the failure of parliamentary democracy in Turkey to provide stability, prosperity or good governance.

The withdrawal of the military from the political arena is likely to be a slow and gradual process, dependent more on changes in the social and political culture and perceived security threats than in the military itself. The massive death toll from the devastating earthquakes of August and November 1999[1] clearly demonstrated to the Turkish public the human cost of a political culture in which bribery, corruption and nepotism have become endemic. Yet by January 2001 the initial wave of public anger had evaporated and reverted to a tendency to wait for changes to be made rather than pressure the authorities into making them. Turkey still has no tradition of political change being driven from below. Nor is there yet any evidence to suggest a change in the social attitudes and practices, particularly the extreme deference to authority and the emphasis on collective rather than individual rights and freedoms, which help perpetuate Turkish political culture. Yet, without such a change, not only will good governance remain elusive but the huge discrepancy in the degree of public esteem in which politicians and the military are held is unlikely to narrow.

The TGS aims eventually to move towards a fully professional military.[2] An end to the concept of a 'citizen army' would inevitably eventually erode the close emotional ties between the military and Turkish society, with profound consequences for public attitudes towards the military. However, in January 2001 the abolition of conscription appeared unlikely in either the short or medium term.[3]

In January 2001 the military continued to insist that the twin threats to Kemalism from Kurdish nationalism and radical Islam had been contained rather than defeated. Privately, some military officials are prepared to countenance a hypothetical relaxation of the expression of a Kurdish identity, such as Kurdish language broadcasting and education, provided that it is contained within a broader Turkish national identity. However, most believe that, for the foreseeable future at least, expressions of Kurdish identity are *per se* a threat to the integrity of the Turkish state.[4]

Nor, particularly while it enjoys the support of the majority of the Turkish public, is the military likely to allow any concessions on the principle of secularism. For the Turkish high command any failure to preserve Ataturk's legacy would be a denial of their *raison d'être*. Yet the new generation of officers graduating from the military academies, who will themselves become generals in approximately 25 years, have received an even more intense grounding than the current high command in the sacred duty of the military to preserve and protect Kemalism; and, despite the recent fragmentation of the Islamist movement, there is still no indication of any decline in either religious sentiment in Turkey or its potential for politicisation.

Turkey's new status as an official candidate for EU membership has, if anything, prompted the military to become more deeply involved in politics as it strives to ensure that legislative changes to fulfil the Copenhagen criteria do not jeopardise its perception of national security. There is also no doubt that even many Turks who support such changes do so not out of conviction but because they see them as a means to an end, namely enabling Turkey to become a member of what is seen as an élite of nations. In January 2001 there was still little awareness in Turkey either of the real cost of EU membership – not least in the erosion of national sovereignty – or that accession remained, at best, a distant prospect, even if restrictions on freedom of speech were abolished and the military withdrew from the political arena.

The EU's November 2000 report on Turkey demonstrated the distance Ankara still has to cover in order to fulfil the Copenhagen criteria.[5] Other candidates, probably – and most critically – including the Republic of Cyprus, are likely to be granted membership long before Turkey. There remains a real danger that, under pressure from Brussels to introduce extensive domestic reforms without any indication of when it may eventually be granted membership,[6] Turkey could experience a nationalist backlash, with the inevitable dire consequences both for domestic political stability and the country's international relations.

Nor is it only Turkey's relations with the EU that are likely to suffer. By January 2001 there were already signs that both NATO and the new US administration would find Turkey a much less acquiescent ally than in the past. The NATO Ministerial Meeting of 14–15 December 2000 was left in disarray by Turkey's refusal to be persuaded by entreaties and blandishments from either the EU or the US to relax its insistence on equal status with EU member states in the decision-process of the ESDP. In early 2001 both the Turkish military and the civilian government still refused even to contemplate making any concessions. On 3 January 2001 Prime Minister Ecevit bluntly declared: 'There is no way we can accept this now or in the future. And in the end the mountain will come to Muhammed.'[7]

On 6 January 2001, shortly after incoming US Secretary of State Colin Powell declared that maintaining the international isolation of Iraqi President Saddam Hussein would be one of the new administration's main foreign policy goals, Turkey announced the appointment of an ambassador to Baghdad for the first time since the 1991 Gulf War.

Turkey's greater assertiveness in foreign policy came amid rising social tensions and political instability at home. A financial crisis in late November 2000 appeared set to trigger an economic slowdown in the first half of 2001, while a spate of attacks by urban left-wing terrorist groups in December 2000 and January 2001 left several policemen dead and led to the most serious outbreak of street fighting between leftists and ultra nationalists since 1980; which in turn increased the pressure on the increasingly fractious and fragile coalition government.

Under such circumstances, the Turkish military is unlikely to be prepared to relinquish the future of the country to its civilian politicians. For the foreseeable future it is likely to remain in the political arena, not so much initiating policy as ensuring that it remains within what the military believes to be acceptable parameters.

Appendix

The Turkish Armed Forces

Total Personnel

Active	609,700[1] (including ε528,000 conscripts)
	Terms of service 18 months
Reserves	378,700 (all to age 41)

Distribution Of Personnel

Army	*Active* ε495,000 (including ε435,000 conscripts)
	Reserves 258,700
Navy	*Active* 54,600 (including 3,100 Marines, 1,050 Coast Guard and 34,500 conscripts)
	Reserves 55,000
Air Force	*Active* 60,100 (including 31,500 conscripts)
	Reserves 65,000

Paramilitary Forces

Gendarmerie	218,000 (Ministry of Interior, Ministry of Defence in war)
Coast Guard	2,200 (including 1,400 conscripts)

[1] All figures taken from The International Institute for Strategic Studies, *The Military Balance 2000–2001* (Oxford: Oxford University Press, 2000), pp. 78–79.

Notes

Introduction

1. The Turkish Republic was officially established on 29 October 1923.
2. This is discussed in greater detail in Chapter One.
3. The military seized power in 1960 and 1980 and forced the removal of the government in 1971 and 1997.
4. 1960–61 and 1980–83.
5. This is discussed in greater detail in Chapter Two.
6. From the Spanish *moderator poder*. See Samuel Finer, *The Man on Horseback: The Role of the Military in Politics* (Boulder: Westview, 1988).
7. Particularly, of course, in Latin America during most of the twentieth century. Juan Rial, 'Armies and Civil Society in Latin America', Larry Diamond and Marc F. Plattner (eds.), *Civil–Military Relations and Democracy* (Baltimore and London: Johns Hopkins University Press, 1996), p. 50.
8. Ordu Yardimlasma Kurumu (Armed Forces Mutual Assistance Fund).
9. Including a joint venture car plant with Renault of France and majority stakes in a 12-branch bank and leasing, factoring and insurance companies.
10. Unlike, for example, China, Pakistan or much of Latin America. Louis W. Goodman, 'Military Roles Past and Present', Diamond and Plattner, *Civil-Military Relations and Democracy*, pp. 31–36.
11. Robert Pinkney, *Right-wing Military Government* (London: Pinter, 1990), p. 14.
12. The impact of the new ideological environment on the Turkish military thus contrasts with, for example, Latin America where the collapse of the ideological threat from communism played a significant role in the withdrawal of the military from politics. The Turkish case also supports Desch's contention that it is a challenging domestic, rather than international, environment which

increases military involvement in politics. Michael C. Desch, *Civilian Control of the Military: The Changing Security Environment* (Baltimore and London: Johns Hopkins University Press, 1999), pp. 1–6 and pp. 97–98.

13 Even in 1980–83, during direct military rule, the junta appointed a civilian, the future prime minister and president Turgut Ozal to control economic policy.

14 The reforms ranged from the introduction of the Latin alphabet and enforcing Western modes of dress to importing new civil, commercial and criminal codes from Europe and even insisting on the building of an opera house in Ankara.

15 Turkey 2000: Turkey's Progress Towards Accession, European Commission. http://www.europa.eu.int/comm/enlargement/dwn/report_11_00/pdf/en/tu

Chapter One

1 The prevalence of such views appears unaffected by the general consensus within both the US and Ankara's European allies that it is in the West's economic, political and strategic interests to have a stable and united Turkey. Nor are they restricted to the general public. In October 2000, Gen. Nahit Senoglu, head of the Military Academies, told the new intake of cadets: 'You will see that Turkey has the most internal and external enemies of any country in the world. You will learn about the dirty aspirations of those who hide behind values such as democracy and human rights and who want to take revenge on

the republic of Ataturk.' Author's translation. Quoted in *Radikal*, 5 October 2000.

2 Albert Howe Lybyer, *The Government of the Ottoman Empire in the Age of Suleiman the Magnificent* (Cambridge: Harvard University Press, 1913), p. 90.

3 David B. Ralston, *Importing the European Army* (London: University of Chicago Press, 1990), p. 43.

4 *Ibid.* p. 56.

5 I. Basgoz and H. E. Wilson, *Educational Problems in Turkey 1920–1940* (Bloomington IND: Indiana University Press, 1986), p. 18.

6 Ralston, *Importing the European Army*, p. 65.

7 Turkey had a single-party system from 1923 to 1946. In 1946 the RPP won the first multiparty elections. But the first fully free multiparty elections were not held until 1950, when they were won by the Democrat Party.

8 Gerassimos Karabelias, 'The Evolution of Civil–Military Relations in Post-war Turkey 1980–95' in Sylvia Kedourie (ed.), *Seventy-Five Years of the Turkish Republic* (London: Frank Cass, 2000), p. 132.

9 In 1961 Menderes and two of his ministers were executed.

10 The Turkish language is based on the addition of suffixes to core nouns and verbs.

11 *Ilkogretim Soysal Bilgiler 5* (Istanbul: Turkish Ministry of Education, 1999), p. 11.

12 *Ibid*, p. 10.

13 *Ibid*, p. 10.

14 *Ibid*, p. 12.

15 *Ibid*, p. 18.

16 *Ibid*, p. 11.

17 *Ibid*, p. 23.

18 *Ibid*, p. 23.

19 Elie Kedourie, *Nationalism*

(London: Hutchinson, 1966), p. 75.

[20] *Ilkogretim Soysal Bilgiler 5*, p. 12.

[21] *Ibid*, p. 21.

[22] *Ibid*, p. 66.

[23] William Hale, *Turkish Politics and the Military* (London: Routledge, 1994), p. 2.

[24] *Anadolu Ajans*, 12 April 1999.

[25] Samuel P. Huntington, 'Reforming Civil–Military Relations', in Diamond and Plattner, *Civil–Military Relations and Democracy*, p. 11.

[26] Unlike, for example, in Russia. See Anatol Lieven, *Chechnya: Tombstone of Russian Power* (New Haven and London: Yale University Press, 1988), pp. 200–201.

[27] For a discussion of the relationship between neo-militaristic displays and nationalism see Hugh Poulton, *Top Hat, Grey Wolf and Crescent* (London: C. Hurst & Co, 1997), p. 9.

[28] Even within the relatively culturally homogenised West, considerable differences still exist in the practice of democracy in, for example, Scandinavia and Greece or the US and France. Nor is there consensus on so-called 'democratic values': the divergence between the EU and the US over capital punishment is just one example.

[29] Serving seven terms as prime minister and another seven-year term as president.

[30] Umit Cizre Sakallioglu, 'Liberalism, Democracy and the Turkish Centre-Right: The Identity Crisis of the True Path Party,' in Sylvia Kedourie (ed.), *Turkey: Identity, Democracy, Politics* (London: Frank Cass, 1998), p. 145.

[31] Over the last decade there has, of course, been a global trend towards a narrowing of ideological differences between parties. In Turkey it has been exacerbated by the clan-like structure of political parties, an inability to institutionalise and a tendency for party leaders to exclude potential rivals from positions of power, with the result that they break away to form their own party.

[32] The 1991 election was won by the True Path Party with 26.2%. The general election of 1995 was won by the Welfare Party with 21.4% and the 1999 elections by the Democratic Left Party with 22.2%.

[33] Figures taken from a compendium of results of opinion polls conducted by Piar-Gallup, *Milliyet*, 8 November 1999.

[34] Opinion poll by Polar Research, *Zaman*, 9 April 2000.

[35] Figures taken from a compendium of results of opinion polls conducted by Piar-Gallup, *Milliyet*, 8 November 1999.

[36] Interviews with parliamentary officials and parliamentarians, Ankara, July 1999.

[37] 'Zafer haftasi yarin basliyor', *Cumhuriyet*, 15 March 1999.

[38] Necati Ozer, *The Principles of Ataturkism* (Istanbul: Beta Basim Yayin, 1995), p. 113.

[39] Criticism of Ataturk is a criminal offence in Turkey, and public discussion of his legacy remains taboo; thus rendering an accurate assessment of support for Kemalism virtually impossible. Explicitly pro-Kemalist parties accounted for around 80% of the votes in the April 1999 elections. Even allowing for a strong Islamist element amongst NAP supporters and, to a lesser extent,

in the MP and the TPP, Kemalists probably still account for at least 65% of the adult population. A confidential opinion poll commissioned by a political party in the run-up to the April 1999 general elections found that around 40% of those questioned were not wholly committed to Kemalism. However, the legal constraints on even asking such questions made it difficult to assess whether those questioned fully understood what they were being asked. The author was shown a copy of the questionnaire and the survey's results in early 1999.

40 *Sosyal Bilgileri Anadolu ve Fen Liselerine Hazirlik* (Istanbul: Surat Basim, 1999), p. 433.
41 Charles H Fairbanks, 'The Postcommunist wars', in Diamond and Plattner, *Civil–Military Relations and Democracy*, p. 148.
42 For a more detailed discussion of this process see Chapter Four.
43 'The increasing loneliness of being Turkey', *The Economist*, 19 July 1997.
44 Compared with the 27% won by the Austrian Freedom Party, whose inclusion in government in February 2000 resulted in Austria's isolation within the EU.
45 Figures taken from a compendium of Piar-Gallup opinion polls, *Milliyet*, 8 November 1999.
46 Meral Gezgin, the chairwoman of the Economic Development Foundation, the leading private sector organisation to promote ties with the EU, 'MUSIAD uyeleri Eris'e ordu-siyaset iliskini sordu', *Milliyet*, 12 February 2000.
47 For example, seditious literature, ranging from advocates of violent Kurdish or left-wing

revolution to calls for Islamist *jihad*, is freely available on the streets even after it has been banned by the courts.
48 Interview with military official, Istanbul, November 1999.
49 Interviews with leftist militants, Istanbul, May 1997.
50 TUSIAD Publication No. T/97–1–212, *Perspectives on Democratisation in Turkey* (Istanbul: TUSIAD, 1997), pp. 87–90.
51 Abdullah Yildiz, *28 Subat Belgeleri* (Istanbul: Pinar Yayinlari, 2000), p. 34.
52 Hale, *Turkish Politics and the Military*, p. 247.
53 Soner Kizilkaya, 'Bir 12 Eylul Bilancosu', *NTV Mag*, September 2000, p. 77.
54 Mehmet Ali Birand, Hikmet Bila, Ridvan Akara, *12 Eylul Turkiye'nin Miladi* (Istanbul: Dogan Kitap, 1999), p. 232.

Chapter Two

1 *Ilkogretim Soysal Bilgiler 5*, (Istanbul: Turkish Ministry of Education, 1999), p. 66.
2 The International Institute for Strategic Studies, *The Military Balance 2000–2001* (Oxford: Oxford University Press, 2000), pp. 78–79.
3 A more detailed breakdown of the respective forces can be found in Appendix A.
4 Col. (ret.) Ismet Polatcan, *Jandarma Kolluk Rehberi* (Istanbul: Polatcan, 1999), p.15.
5 Interview with military official, April 1999.
6 Interviews with expelled officers, Istanbul, June 1997.
7 Hale, *Turkish Politics and the Military*, p. 320.
8 Semih Vaner, 'The Army' in Irvin

Cemil Schick and Ertugrul Ahmet Tonak (eds.), *Turkey in Transition* (Oxford: Oxford University Press, 1987), p. 243.

[9] Interview with Gen. (ret.) Muhittin Fisunoglu, Istanbul, October 1999.

[10] Interview with military official, February 1999.

[11] Equivalent to captain and admiral respectively in the navy

[12] Article 30, Turkish Armed Forces Personnel Law No. 926, Amendment 3909/1 of 6 May 1993, 27 July 1967. Justice Ministry web site. http://www.adalet.gov.tr

[13] Interview with retired military official, Istanbul, September 1999.

[14] Clause 11 of Law No 353 on the Establishment and Functioning of Military Courts. http://www.adalet.gov.tr

[15] Clause 159 of the Turkish Criminal Code makes insulting 'Turkishness', the Turkish state, its parliament, ministries and security forces punishable by up to six years in prison. The maximum jail term can be raised to nine years if a Turk insults 'Turkishness' while in a foreign country. Polatcan, *Jandarma Kolluk Rehberi*, p. 653. Traditionally, the Turkish military has vigorously pursued incitements to avoid military service but has usually been content to leave prosecution of alleged defamations of the armed forces to pro-military members of the civilian judiciary.

[16] Interview with military official, December 1999.

[17] Visit to Commando Training Centre, Egridir, May 1998.

[18] Interview with Adm. (ret.) Tanzar Dincer, Ankara, July 1998.

[19] Interview with military official, Istanbul, October 1998.

[20] Interviews with expelled officers, Istanbul, June 1997.

[21] Gen. Huseyin Kivrikoglu quoted in 'Hukumete asker testi', *Radikal*, 31 August 2000.

[22] Interview with Gen. (ret.) Dogan Beyazit, Istanbul, March 1998.

[23] Particularly supporters of Islamist sect leader Fetullah Gulen, see Chapter Four.

[24] Interviews with expelled officers, Istanbul, March 1999.

[25] In its 2000 annual report Amnesty International stated that in Turkey: 'Torture mainly occurred in police or *gendarmerie* custody.' *Amnesty International Annual Report 2000*, http://www.web.amnesty.org/web/ar2000web.nsf. Similarly, almost all of the cases of human-rights violations cited in a report by the Turkish Studies Centre in the Netherlands also involve the police or *gendarmerie* rather than the regular army. *Turkiye'de Ordu ve Insan Haklari Ihlalleri* (Amsterdam: Turkiye Incelemeleri Merkezi, 1999), pp. 12–26. Of the 649 victims of torture treated at the Turkish Human Rights Foundation rehabilitation centres in 1999, 454 had been tortured inside police stations or *gendarmerie* interrogation centres, while 195 had been tortured elsewhere, almost all by police, *gendarmerie* or prison guards. *Tedavi ve Rehabilitasyon Merkezleri Raporu 1999* (Ankara: Turkish Human Rights Foundation, 2000), p. 28.

[26] Conversations with serving officers, south-east Turkey, February and July 1998.

[27] Fikri Saglar and Emin Ozgonul, *Kod adi Susurluk* (Istanbul: Boyut Kitaplari, 1998), p. 390.

[28] e.g. Amnesty International, 'Evidence of persecution of

conscripts on the increase', EUR 44/055/1999, 27 August 1999, http://www.web.amnesty.org/ai.nsf/Index/EUR440551999

[29] 'These things do happen from time to time but it is up to us to deal with them.' Author's translation. Interview with military official, December 1999.

[30] Mehmet Ali Birand, *Shirts of Steel* (London: I. B. Tauris, 1991), p. 44.

[31] Interview with Adm. (ret.) Tanzar Dincer, Ankara, July 1998.

[32] *Ibid.*

[33] Military academy web site, http://www.kho.edu.tr

[34] *Ibid.*

[35] Interview with Gen. (ret.) Muhittin Fisunoglu, Istanbul, July 1999. See also Birand, *Shirts of Steel*, p. 54.

[36] Birand, *Shirts of Steel*, p. 52, and *Anadolu Ajans*, 13 March 1999.

[37] Visit to Turkish military academy, May 1998.

[38] Hale, *Turkish Politics and the Military*, p. 200.

[39] Birand, *Shirts of Steel*, p. 58.

[40] 'Kara Kuvvetlerinin 2206'nci Yildonumu Kutlandi', *Kara Kuvvetleri Haber Bulletin*, Year 3, Issue 9, July 1997, p. 2.

[41] Visit to Turkish General Staff headquarters, Ankara, February 1998.

[42] Turkish Armed Forces web site, http://www.tsk.mil.tr

[43] Rohan Butler and J. P. T. Bury (eds.), *Documents on British Foreign Policy 1919–1939, First Series, Volume XV* (London: Her Majesty's Stationery Office, 1967), pp. 174–181.

[44] Turkish Armed Forces web site, http://www.tsk.mil.tr

[45] *Ibid.*

[46] For a more detailed discussion of the military's legal obligations see Chapter Three.

[47] Article 35 of Turkish Armed Forces Internal Service Law of January 1961 states that it is the duty of the Turkish Armed Forces to 'protect and preserve' the Turkish republic. See Chapter Three.

[48] Chief of staff, Gen. Kivrikoglu, TGS Press Office, Announcement No. 30, 17 March 2000. Turkish Armed Forces web site, http://www.tsk.mil.tr

[49] Chief of staff Gen. Huseyin Kivrikoglu's message on the seventy-sixth anniversary of the foundation of the Turkish republic. Author's translation. *Anadolu Ajans*, 29 October 1999.

[50] Birand, *Shirts of Steel*, p. 69.

[51] Andrew Mango, *Ataturk* (London: John Murray, 1999), p. 400.

[52] D. A. Rustow, 'The Army In The Founding Of The Turkish Republic', *World Politics 11*, July 1959, p. 550.

[53] Carolina G. Hernandez, 'Controlling Asia's Armed Forces', in Diamond and Plattner, *Civil-Military Relations and Democracy*, p. 71.

[54] S. E. Finer, 'Retreat to barracks: notes on the practice and theory of military withdrawal from seats of power', *Third World Quarterly* Vol. 7 No. 1, 1985, p. 25.

[55] Dr Rebecca Durrant, 'The Military in Turkish Politics', *Mediterranean Politics*, Volume 2 No 2, 1997.

[56] Ihsan D. Dagi, 'Democratic Transition in Turkey, 1980–83: The Impact of European Diplomacy', in Kedourie, *Turkey: Identity, Democracy, Politics*, p. 139.

[57] See 'The Place of the Turkish Armed Forces in Society', Turkish Armed Forces web site, http://www.tsk.mil.tr

[58] Chief of staff Gen. Huseyin

Kivrikoglu, Turkish General Staff Statement No. 30, 17 March 2000. http://www.tsk.mil.tr

[59] Interview with Adm. (ret.) Tanzar Dincer, Ankara, July 1998.

[60] Pinkney, *Right-Wing Military Government*, p. 99.

[61] Interview with Gen. (ret.) Dogan Beyazit, Istanbul, March 1998.

[62] Deputy chief of staff Gen. Cevik Bir, 21 February 1997, quoted in Yildiz, *28 Subat Belgeleri*, p. 31.

[63] Feroz Ahmad, *The Making of Modern Turkey* (London: Routledge, 1993), p. 9.

[64] Interview with military official, December 1999.

[65] D. Lerner and R. D. Robinson, 'Swords into ploughshares; the Turkish army as a modernising force', *World Politics 13*, October 1960, p. 28.

[66] Ahmad, *The Making of Modern Turkey*, p. 125.

[67] Interview with military official, June 1999.

[68] Sydney Nettleton Fisher, 'The Role of the Military in Society and Government in Turkey', *The Military in the Middle East: Problems in Society and Government* (Columbus OH: Ohio State University Press, 1963), pp. 31–32.

[69] Hale, *Turkish Politics and the Military*, p. 93.

[70] Interview with military official, April 1999.

[71] Ahmad, *The Making of Modern Turkey*, p. 124.

[72] Dr Umit Ozdag, *Menderes Doneminde Ordu-Siyaset Iliskileri ve 27 Mayis Ihtilali* (Istanbul: Boyut Kitaplari, 1997), p.56.

[73] Hale, *Turkish Politics and the Military*, p. 131.

[74] Interview with retired military official serving at the time, Istanbul, September 1999.

[75] Gurcan on 27 June 1964 and

Aydemir on 4 July 1964.

[76] Birand, *Shirts of Steel*, p. 36.

[77] Walter F Weiker, *The Turkish Revolution 1960–1961* (Washington DC: Brookings Institution, 1963), p. 80.

[78] Erik J. Zurcher, *Turkey: A Modern History* (London: I. B. Tauris, 1993), p. 270.

[79] Mehmet Ali Birand, Can Dundar, Bulent Capli, *12 Mart* (Istanbul: Imge Kitabevi, 1994), p. 208.

[80] *Ibid*, p. 209.

[81] Nazli Ilicak, *12 Mart Cuntalari* (Istanbul: Tercuman, 1986), p. 5.

[82] Muhsin Batur, *Anilar ve Gorusler* (Istanbul: Milliyet Yayinlari, 1985), p. 299.

[83] Hale, *Turkish Politics and the Military*, p. 186.

[84] Henri J. Barkey and Graham E. Fuller, *Turkey's Kurdish Question* (Maryland: Rowman & Littlefield, 1998), p. 22.

[85] C. H. Dodd, *The Crisis of Turkish Democracy* (Cambridge: Eothen, 1990), p. 24.

[86] Gen. (ret.) Kenan Evren, *Ne Demislerdi? Ne Dediler? Ne Diyorlar?* (Istanbul: Milliyet Kitaplari, 1997), p. 12.

[87] Birand, Bila, Akara, *12 Eylul Turkiye'nin Miladi*, p. 165.

[88] Mehmet Ali Birand, *The Generals' Coup* (London: Brassey's Defence Publishers, 1987), p. 195.

[89] Interview with military official, November 1999.

[90] Ahmad, *The Making of Modern Turkey*, p. 183.

[91] Mehmet Semih Gemalmaz, 'Ceberrut Bir Rejim Miras Kaldi', *NTV Mag*, September 2000, p.55.

[92] Hale, *Turkish Politics and the Military*, p. 295.

[93] 'There are two things which could prompt another coup; *sharia* and the Kurdish problem.' Gen. Kenan Evren, 21 March 1991, quoted in Cuneyt

Arcayurek, *Buyuklere Masallar, Kucuklere Gercekler Vol. 3* (Istanbul: Bilgi Yayinevi, 2000), p. 310.
94 Hale, *Turkish Politics and the Military*, p. 292.
95 Arcayurek, *Buyuklere Masallar, Kucuklere Gercekler Vol. 3*, p. 115.
96 Interview with Gen. (ret.) Muhittin Fisunoglu, September 1999.
97 Interview with retired subordinate of Gen. Dogan Gures, Istanbul, May 1999.
98 Fehmi Koru, *One Column Ahead* (Istanbul: Timas Publications, 2000), p. 176.

Chapter Three

1 Hale, *Turkish Politics and the Military*, p. 80.
2 Preamble, Turkish Constitution, Turkish Ministry of Foreign Affairs web site, http://www.mfa.gov.tr
3 Preamble, Turkish Constitution, MFA web site http://www.mfa.gov.tr
4 Article 4, Turkish Constitution, MFA web site http://www.mfa.gov.tr
5 Tuncer Ozyavuv, *Osmanli-Turk Anayasalari* (Aklim Yayinevi, 1997), pp. 170–171 and pp. 271–272.
6 Niyazi Berkes, *The Development of Secularism In Turkey* (London: Hurst & Company, 1964), p. 461.
7 Article 3, 1961 Constitution, Ozyavuv, *Osmanli-Turk Anayasalari*, p. 171.
8 Article 3, 1961 Constitution, Ozyavuv, *Osmanli-Turk Anayasalari*, p. 279 and p. 223 respectively.
9 Article 131, Turkish Constitution, Turkish Ministry of Foreign Affairs web site http://
www.mfa.gov.tr
10 Interview with high-ranking military official, July 1999.
11 Interview with high-ranking military official, October 1999.
12 Author's translation. Justice Ministry web site. http://www.adalet.gov.tr
13 Author's translation. Gen. (ret.) Nevzat Bolugiray, *28 Subat Sureci* (Istanbul: Tekin Yayinevi, 1999), p. 167.
14 Article 118, Turkish Constitution, MFA web site http://www.mfa.gov.tr
15 Author's translation. Article 111, 1961 Turkish Constitution, Tuncer Ozyavuv, *Osmanli-Turk Anayasalari* (Kocaeli: Aklim Yayinevi, 1997), p. 224.
16 Turkish Constitution, MFA web site http://www.mfa.gov.tr
17 Turkish Constitution, MFA web site http://www.mfa.gov.tr
18 Author's translation. Article 2a, National Security Council Law No. 2945, Justice Ministry web site, http://www.adalet.gov.tr
19 Article 11, National Security Council Law No 2945, Justice Ministry web site, http://www.adalet.gov.tr
20 Author's translation. Article 2b, National Security Council Law No. 2945, Justice Ministry web site, http://www.adalet.gov.tr
21 The president, prime minister, foreign minister, defence minister and interior minister.
22 Ertugrul Ozturk, 'Milli eylem stratejisi belgesi', *Hurriyet*, 24 June 1999.
23 Bolugiray, *28 Subat Sureci*, p. 54.
24 *Ibid* p. 55.
25 The other two parties were the nationalist-left Democratic Left Party (DLP) and the centre-right Democratic Turkey Party (DTP).
26 Not that this was a new idea. See Ambassador (ret.) Sukru

Elekdag, '2½ War Strategy', *Perceptions Vol 1*, March–May 1996, p. 33.

[27] Visit to artillery training school, May 1998.

[28] Bolugiray, *28 Subat Sureci*, p. 56.

[29] The impact of the military on different policy areas is examined in more detail in Chapter Four.

[30] Deniz Kuvvetleri Komutanligi'nin 1 Mayis 1997 gun ve ISTH: 3429-1-9/IKK.S. (307), quoted in Yildiz, *28 Subat Belgeleri*, pp. 132–133.

[31] Article 5, National Security Council Law No 2945, Justice Ministry web site, http://www.adalet.gov.tr

[32] Interview with Gen. (ret.) Dogan Beyazit, former National Security Council general secretary, Istanbul, March 1998.

[33] Repercussions of this speech by First Army Commander Gen. Atilla Ates are discussed in greater detail in Chapter Four.

[34] For example, chief of staff, Gen. Huseyin Kivrikoglu's briefing of 3 September 1999, Ismet Berkan, 'Kivrikoglu her seyi anlatti', *Radikal*, 4 September 1999.

[35] Interview with military official, September 1997.

[36] Vural Savas, *Irtica ve Boluculuge Karsi Militan Demokrasi* (Ankara: Bilgi Yayinevi, 2000).

[37] Article 143, Turkish Constitution. Turkish Ministry of Foreign Affairs web site http://www.mfa.gov.tr

[38] Amendment to Article 143 of Turkish Constitution, *Official Gazette* of 18 June 2000, Turkish Grand National Assembly web site http://www.tbmm.gov.tr

[39] For example, Neil Hicks, Lawyers Committee on Human Rights senior program coordinator, 'Testimony to the Commission on Security and Cooperation in Europe', 18 March 1999.

[40] For example, ECHR Decision No. 933, of 9 June 1998 in the case of Incal vs Turkey, which ruled that the presence of a military judge was 'in violation of the principle of the independence and impartiality of the judiciary, safeguarded by Article 6 of the European Convention on Human Rights.' ECHR web site. http://www.echr.coe.int/

[41] Interviews with members of the Istanbul Bar Association, June–July 2000.

[42] Interview with Ministry of Foreign Affairs official, December 1999.

[43] Refik Baydur, *Bizimcete* (Istanbul: Cem Ofset, 2000), p 49.

Chapter Four

[1] For example, in 1997 the TGS succeeded in instigating the downfall of the Islamist-led government, but three and a half years later less than one-third of the 18 anti-Islamist measures proposed at the 28 February 1997 NSC meeting had been implemented.

[2] The military dominance of the DIEC was clearly demonstrated in 1998 when the civilian government abolished a defence fund levy on petroleum products. The DIEC, which is ostensibly headed by the prime minister, protested the decision, arguing that it would restrict funds and could delay several important defence programmes. But the civilian government, also headed by the prime minister, defended it on the grounds that it needed to stabilise petrol pump prices and reduce

inflationary pressures.

[3] Interview with military official, October 1999.

[4] One reason appears to have been increasing distrust of civilian governments, particularly after the WP's 1995 election victory, although the military was also concerned about political considerations affecting the equipment purchases. For example, in 1995 the then prime minister Tansu Ciller agreed to buy 30 *Cougar* utility helicopters from the Franco-German Eurocopter consortium in an attempt to secure French backing for Turkey's Customs Union agreement with the EU; despite protests from the TGS, which believed that the US Sikorsky's *Black Hawks* were a superior platform.

[5] Prime minister 1983–89 and president 1989–93.

[6] In the period 1990–99 annual retail inflation averaged 78.8%.

[7] In the most recent census of 1997, 30% of the Turkish population was under the age of 15. Turkish State Institute of Statistics, 1997 census results.

[8] In the early 1990s WP leaders were quite clear in their intentions. In 1994 the WP submitted a proposal in parliament to amend the constitutional provisions on secularism to allow for 'multiple legal-orders' on the basis of religious belief similar to those reportedly applied by the Prophet Mohammed in seventh century Medina. *Refah Partisi'nin Anayasa Degisikligi Uzlasma Teklifi* (Ankara: Welfare Party, 1994). In 1993 Tayyip Erdogan, later the WP mayor of Istanbul, declared: 'There is no room for Kemalism or for any other official ideology

in Turkey's future.' Interview with Erdogan in Metin Sever and Cem Dizdar (eds.), 2. *Cumhuriyet Tartismalari* (Ankara: Basak Yainlari, 1993), p 425. While leading WP ideologue Abdurrahman Dilipak bluntly declared. 'Democracy is the Trojan horse of Western cultural imperialism.' Abdurrahman Dilipak, *Sorular, Sorunlar ve Cevaplar* (Istanbul: Beyan Yayinlar, 1993), p. 93.

[9] Prime minister's message to mark the Islamic Feast of the Sacrifice, quoted in *Dunya*, 16 March 2000.

[10] For example, the growth of Koranic schools and courses, many of which advocated *sharia* law, was allowed to continue unchecked. Graduates from these schools played a significant role in the rapid rise in the Islamist vote during the 1990s.

[11] Elisabeth Ozdalga, *The Veiling Issue, Official Secularism and Popular Islam in Modern Turkey* (London: Curzon, Nordic Institute of Asia Studies Report Series No. 33, 1998), p. 43.

[12] Interview with military official, June 1996.

[13] The then defence minister, Turhan Tayan cited this as the catalyst for the process that culminated on 28 February 1997, *Milliyet*, 28 February 2000.

[14] Author's translation. Adm. (ret.) Salim Dervisoglu interviewed by Sedat Ergin, 'O gece Golcuk'te neler konutuk', *Hurriyet*, 3 November 1999.

[15] Sedat Ergin, 'Sincan yolunu hindi acti', *Hurriyet*, 24 August 1997.

[16] Hulki Cevizoglu, *28 Subat Bir Hukumet Nasil Devrildi* (Istanbul: Beyaz Yayinlari, 1998), p. 31. Bekir was sentenced to three years and nine months in prison

on 16 October 1997.

[17] Yildiz, *28 Subat Belgeleri*, p. 32.

[18] Faik Bulut, *Islamci Orgutleri* (Istanbul: Tumzamanlar Yayincilik, 1994), p. 707.

[19] 'Turkish stocks climb on uneventful National Security Council meeting', *Bridge News*, 31 March 1997.

[20] Then interior minister, Meral Aksener speaking to Hakan Akpinar, *Hurriyet*, 1 March 2000.

[21] Erbakan finally added his signature to the declaration on 6 March 1997.

[22] Interviews with WP officials, 20–21 March 1997.

[23] Interview with leading trade union official, April 1997.

[24] Interview with leftist extremists, May 1997.

[25] 'If it comes down to the wire, then there will be a coup. There is no other option.' Author's translation. Gen. (ret.) Dogan Beyazit, adviser to chief of staff Gen. Hakki Karadayi, quoted in 'Halk isterse darbe olur', *Yeni Yuzyil*, 29 April 1997.

[26] Baydur, *Bizim Cete*, p 49.

[27] Sukru Elekdag, 'Hesaplasma', *Milliyet*, 19 May 1997.

[28] 'Helikopteri PKK dusurdu', *Milliyet*, 7 June 1997.

[29] Interviews with military officials, July 1997.

[30] Interview with military official, September 1997.

[31] Interviews with sources close to the negotiations, autumn 1997.

[32] Nuri Sefa Erdem, 'Yilmaz: BCG artik gereksiz', *Yeni Yuzyil*, 11 September 1997.

[33] Interview with military official, Istanbul, October 1999.

[34] *Turkish Daily News*, 21 March 1998.

[35] Interview with an aide to Yilmaz, Istanbul, April 1998.

[36] Stephen Kinzer, 'Turkish Duel Over Islam Seems to Fade', *New York Times*, 20 August 1998.

[37] 'Irticaya karsi kurtulus savasi baslatilmali', *Dunya*, 9 January 1999.

[38] Mesut Yilmaz, quoted in Osman Aydogan, 'Askerler Sikistiriyor', *Radikal*, 9 September 2000.

[39] 'Ecevit'den uc uyari', *Radikal*, 4 February 1999.

[40] Closed by the Constitutional Court on 16 January 1998, see Chapter Three.

[41] Interview with military official, May 2000.

[42] Interview with military official, September 1999.

[43] Sedat Ergin, 'Askerden 12 mesaj', *Hurriyet*, 4 September 1999.

[44] Gulen has been in self-imposed exile in the US since early 1999, ostensibly for medical treatment, but his followers still control a vast network of companies, Islamist financial institutions, media outlets and over 400 schools, of which approximately half are in Turkey and the remainder abroad, mostly in Central Asia. Ismet Demirdogen, 'Irtica'nin okul raporu', *Radikal*, 1 September 1999.

[45] Most of the officers expelled for Islamist sympathies were alleged to have links to Gulen's sect. Interviews with military officials, 1998 and 1999.

[46] 'Asker surekli uyariyordu', *Radikal*, 21 June 1999.

[47] For example, Ecevit hosted Gulen at his private residence in July 1998. 'Fetullah Hoca Temmuz 1998'de Ecevit'in evindeydi', *Hurriyet*, 23 July 1999.

[48] 'Erkaya'nin uyarisini Ecevit dikkate almadi', *Sabah*, 26 February 2000.

[49] 'Komutan demisse dogrudur', *Milliyet*, 1 September 2000.

[50] Yildiz, *28 Subat Belgeleri*, p. 96.

51 *Ibid.*, p. 42.

52 'Hukumete asker testi', *Radikal*, 31 August 2000. No such law had been passed by the end of December 2000.

53 The Constitutional Court was expected to rule on Savas' application for the closure of the VP in November 2000.

54 'Tarihsel Donemec', *Cumhuriyet*, 28 February 2000.

55 By the end of October 2000 only a handful of Turkish Islamist groups had resorted to violence, without much success; although Turkish intelligence reports suggested that over 10,000 members of various groups had undergone some form of arms training. The two most important groups were the Islamic Raiders of the Greater Eastern Front (IBDA-C) and *Ilim*. During the mid-1990s IBDA-C grew to perhaps 200–300 militants. But it mainly confined itself to attacking symbols of Kemalism, such as destroying statues of Ataturk. By late 2000 most of its leaders had been imprisoned and its networks crippled, if not destroyed. The *Ilim* Group was far more powerful, although until the 1990s it had confined itself to the south-east. Its policy of assassinating members of the theoretically atheistic PKK, resulted in a considerable degree of tolerance, if not collusion, on the part of the local police and gendarmerie. However, its network was rolled up when it attempted to move into major cities in the West and target moderate Turkish Islamists.

56 'Turkey's Divided Islamists', *Strategic Comments*, Volume 6 Issue 3, The International Institute for Strategic Studies, April 2000.

57 Turkish General Staff Statement No 1, 24 January 2000, Turkish Armed Forces web site, http://www.tsk.mil.tr

58 In late 2000 the VP was deeply divided between the older generation, who looked to Erbakan for leadership, and younger Islamists, such as former Istanbul Mayor Tayyip Erdogan.

59 Interview with Islamist extremists, September 1999.

60 Author's translation. Turkish General Staff Statement No 2., 26 January 2000, Turkish Armed Forces web site http://www.tsk.mil.tr

61 Visits to south-east Turkey, 1990–1993.

62 The precise number of burned and evacuated settlements is unclear. Amnesty International estimates that 3,000 settlements had been destroyed by summer 1999, the majority by the *gendarmerie* (Amnesty International, 'Evidence of persecution of conscripts on the increase', EUR 44/055/1999, 27 August 1999, http://www.web.amnesty.org/ai.nsf/Index/EUR440551999). The Turkish Parliamentary Migration Commission reported that 3,428 villages and hamlets had been destroyed by the beginning of 1997 (*Radikal*, 17 January 1997). While the Turkish Human Rights Association gives a figure of 3,246 for the period 1989–1998 (Vedat Cetin, *Yakilan/Bosaltilan Koyler ve Goc*, Ankara: Insan Haklari Dernegi, 1999, p. 61.).

63 Interviews with military officials, Sirnak, February 1998.

64 *Ic Guvenlikte Halkla Iliskiler ve Halkin Kazanilmasi: Davranis Ilkeleri Rehberi* (Ankara: Turkish General Staff, 1995).

[65] This is discussed in greater detail in the section on Foreign Policy.

[66] During the early 1990s PKK militants had usually preferred to fight to the death, fearing (not without justification if they fell into the hands of the Special Teams or were interrogated by the police or *gendarmerie*) that they would be tortured or executed if they were captured. In the mid-1990s the TGS launched a vigorous propaganda campaign, mostly in the form of leaflets, reassuring the militants of fair treatment if they laid down their arms.

[67] Turkish Armed Forces web site. http://www.tsk.mil.tr/tsk/basin/bbm/gnkur/g11.html.

[68] Henri J. Barkey and Graham E. Fuller, *Turkey's Kurdish Question* (Maryland: Rowman & Littlefield, 1998), p. 141.

[69] Interviews with PKK militants, south-east Turkey, October 1990 and April 1991.

[70] Interview with Gen. (ret.) Muhittin Fisunoglu, Istanbul, September 1999.

[71] For example, 'Military force is not enough to combat terrorism. Economic and social measures are also needed.' Author's translation of interview with chief of staff Gen. Hakki Karadayi in 'Ordu da sosyal onlem istedi', *Radikal*, 25 December 1996.

[72] Entitled 'Nation-Army: Hand-in-Hand'. Metin Okcu, 'Civil affairs support by military to Southeast Anatolia', *National Strategy*, September–October 2000, pp. 34–39.

[73] Interviews with military officials, August, October 1999.

[74] Ismet Berkan, 'Kivrikoglu her sey anlatti', *Radikal*, 4 September 1999.

[75] Interviews with sources close to the military, April 1995.

[76] Kemal Kirisci and Gareth Winrow, *The Turkish Question and Turkey* (London: Cass, 1997), p. 138.

[77] Leyla Boulton, 'Turkish plan to lift south-east', *Financial Times*, 17 February 2000.

[78] Adnan Keskin, 'Kopenhag'a MGK serhi', *Radikal*, 14 June 2000.

[79] Adnan Keskin, 'MGK'nin dedigi oldu', *Radikal*, 23 June 2000.

[80] 'Evaluation of the Internal Security Operations 2000', quoted in 'Kurtce TV'ye Fren', *Radikal*, 8 December 2000.

[81] The TGS has reservations about how and when Kurdish broadcasting should be permitted rather than objecting to it in principle. For example, officers candidly admit that they would prefer Kurdish broadcasting on state-controlled television to Kurds continuing to receive satellite broadcasts of the pro-PKK Medya TV. Former Navy Commander Adm. (ret.) Salim Dervisoglu speaking with Utku Cakirozer, 'Kutce TV Yarali', *Hurriyet*, 1 December 2000.

[82] 'Kurtce TV'ye Fren', *Radikal*, 8 December 2000.

[83] Author's translation. *Kanal D News*, 17 March 1999.

[84] 'IMKB Kivrikoglu'yla cesaretlendi', *Finansal Forum*, 19 March 1999.

[85] Interviews with military officials March, April 1999.

[86] Turkish presidents are elected by parliament from candidates nominated by parliamentarians.

[87] Author's translation from a speech by chief of staff, Gen. Huseyin Kivrikoglu to the Association to Combat Corruption on 11 April 2000,

quoted in 'Ciddi ve saibesiz', *Hurriyet*, 12 April 2000.

[88] Interviews with sources close to Yilmaz, Ankara, August 1999 and Istanbul, January 2000.

[89] Interview with sources close to the military, April 2000.

[90] 'Askerin aday tarifi', *Radikal*, 16 April 2000.

[91] 'Asker habersizdi', *Radikal*, 26 April 2000.

[92] Unlike any other ministry, the Ministry of Foreign Affairs remained virtually immune to penetration by Islamists even during the WP–TPP coalition. Interviews with members of the civil service, Ankara, March 1997 and December 1999.

[93] Interview with military official, February 1998.

[94] Interviews with Ministry of Foreign Affairs officials, December 1999.

[95] 'Sinir asan sulara 3 asamali plan', *Cumhuriyet*, 15 January 1999.

[96] Tuncay Ozkan, *Operasyon* (Istanbul: Dogan Kitapcilik, 2000), p. 105.

[97] Author's translation. 'Org. Ates: sabrimiz kalmidi', *Radikal*, 17 September 1998.

[98] Interview with military official, October 1998.

[99] Fikret Bila, 'Asker emir bekliyor', *Milliyet*, 3 October 1998.

[100] Interviews with military officials, November and December 1998.

[101] Minutes of Meeting (unofficial translation), Ministry of Foreign Affairs, Ankara.

[102] Author's translation. Yildiz, *28 Subat Belgeleri*, p. 96.

[103] 'Komuntandan savas uyarisi', *Milliyet*, 29 June 2000.

[104] Interview with source close to the military, July 2000.

[105] Mainly because of the economic costs of the closure of the pipeline carrying Iraqi oil to Yumurtalik on the Turkish Mediterranean coast and the loss of most of the once lucrative border trade between south-east Turkey and northern Iraq.

[106] Interviews with Ministry of Foreign Affairs officials, Ankara, July and December 1999.

[107] Interview with military official, March 1997.

[108] Turkey formally recognised the Palestinian right to statehood on 15 November 1988.

[109] Interview with military official, March 1997.

[110] 'Israeli companies' concerns over defense tenders grow', *Turkish Daily News*, 16 August 2000.

[111] Israeli Military Industries for the $350m upgrade of 170 M-60 tanks and Israeli Aerospace Industries for a $274m project to launch a military observation satellite. 'Israeli companies' concerns over defense tenders grow', *Turkish Daily News*, 16 August 2000.

[112] For example, the *Arrow*-2 project mentioned above.

[113] Gen. (ret.) Cevik Bir, 'Guvenlik acisindan AB ve Turkiye', *National Strategy*, March–April 2000, pp. 19–21.

[114] Interview with source close to military, September 2000.

[115] Gil Hofman, 'Armenian genocide to be taught', *Jerusalem Post*, 25 April 2000.

[116] 'Misilleme basladi', *Sabah*, 5 October 2000. The TGS also suspended all ongoing negotiations with US defence firms, and the Turkish government sent a planeload of aid to Baghdad in a calculated signal to Washington that its loyalty in abiding by UN sanctions could not be taken for granted. Pressure from the Pentagon and the Clinton administration subsequently

secured the indefinite postponement of the presentation of the
resolution for full Congressional
approval. 'A Relief For Turkey
For The Time Being', *Turkish
Probe*, 23 October 2000.

[117] Interview with military official,
June 1999.

[118] Interviews with military officials,
May 1998.

[119] For example,: 'The West has
developed a specific term for its
conduct towards Turkey. They
describe it as "an acceptable
instability". I think it is more
appropriate to call it "a
controllable instability".'
Author's translation. Former
head of the military academies,
Gen. (ret.) Kemal Yavuz,
interviewed in Hakanturk, *Asrin
Operasyonu* (Istanbul: Atlantik
Yayinlari, 1999), p. 108.

[120] Interview with Gen. (ret.)
Muhittin Fisunoglu, Istanbul,
September 1999.

[121] The agreement was signed in
March 1995, ratified by the
European Parliament in
December the same year and
came into force in January 1996.

[122] Interview with Adm. (ret) Guven
Erkaya, Istanbul, October 1998.

[123] Interview with Ministry of
Foreign Affairs official, January
1997.

[124] Ertugrul Ozkok, 'Gürel'in ege
ordusu cevabý', *Hurriyet*, 23 May
2000.

[125] Author's translation. Turkish
General Staff Statement No. 8, 23
May 2000, Turkish Armed Forces
web site, http://www.tsk.mil.tr

[126] Interview with military official,
November 1999.

[127] Interview with retired TRNC
official, northern Cyprus,
November 1999.

[128] Survey conducted by the Cypriot
Public Opinion and Market

Research Company (COMAR),
quoted in 'Entegrasyona hayir',
Radikal, 8 September 2000.

[129] Yusuf Kanli and Huseyin Alkan,
'KKTC-Turkey row over army's
role', *Turkish Daily News*, 5 July
2000.

[130] Sener Levent of the left-wing
daily *Avrupa*.

[131] Ceyda Karan, 'Kabe'nin
golgesinde bir devletcik', *Radikal*,
17 July 2000.

[132] Interviews with Ministry of
Foreign Affairs and government
officials, January and March
1997.

[133] Interviews with military officials,
March and July 1997.

[134] Foreign and Turkish journalists
were invited to watch special
forces lay charges against
replicas of the S-300s before
calling in an air strike by F-16
fighter-bombers. 'Turkey still
watchful over Cyprus', *Turkish
Probe No. 252*, 7 November 1997,
pp. 2–3.

[135] 'Turkey still watchful over
Cyprus', *Turkish Probe No. 252*, 7
November 1997, pp. 2–3.

[136] 'Genelkurmay'da Kibris alarmi',
Milliyet, 18 June 1998.

[137] Interview with military official,
October 1998.

[138] Interviews with Ministry of
Foreign Affairs officials and
members of the government,
December 1999.

[139] Of course, one of the ironies of
the Turkish military's repeated
commitment to Westernisation is
that to most EU countries the
withdrawal of the military from
politics is a precondition for
Turkey being accepted as a
Westernised state.

[140] Interview with military official,
December 1999.

[141] Metin Toker, 'Idamin kalkasina
asker karsi degil', Milliyet, 21

June 2000.

142 'Let there be 100 civilian members if necessary.' Author's translation. Gen. Kivrikoglu, quoted in Serpil Cevikcan, 'MGK genisleyebilir', *Milliyet*, 25 July 2000.

143 Kemal Ilter, 'MGK snag in Copenhagen criteria', *Turkish Daily News*, 24 June 2000.

144 Author's translation. Gen. (ret) Cevik Bir, 'How we can become a member of the EU', *National Strategy*, July–August 2000, pp. 30-31.

145 Author's translation. Speech at Gulhane Military Medical Academy (GATA), 9 October 2000, quoted in 'AB zorunlu, ama …', *Milliyet*, 10 October 2000.

Conclusion

1 The official death tolls from the Izmit earthquake of 17 August 1999 and Bolu earthquake of 12 November 1999 are 17 and 842 respectively. However, the real death toll is believed to have been at least 25,000, perhaps 30,000, almost all the direct result of the failure to enforce safety standards or building regulations.

2 Metin Okcu, 'Profesyonel askerlige dogru', *National Strategy*, November–December 1999, pp. 26–28.

3 In December 2000 the MND dismissed proposals for even a reduction in military service on the grounds that the supply of conscripts was only just sufficient to meet the military's requirements. MND general secretary, Col. Tamer Buyukkantarcioglu quoted in 'Milli Savunma bedelliye karsi', *Radikal*, 10 December 2000

4 'If our European friends come to us and say that the era of the nation state is over and that we should abandon the idea, we shall tell them that we can never even discuss this, much less accept it.' Gen. Nahit Senogul, head of the military academies. Author's translation. Quoted in *Radikal*, 13 January 2001.

5 Turkey 2000: Turkey's Progress Towards Accession, European Commission. http://www.europa.eu.int/comm/enlargement/dwn/report_11_00/pdf/en/tu

6 In late December 2000 there was little realisation in Turkey of the full implications of the often fraught discussions over enlargement at the EU Summit in Nice, which were predicated on the EU taking in up to 12 new members; while Turkey is 13th in line

7 'Ecevit: EU has nothing to fear from Turkey', *Turkish Daily News*, 4 January 2001.